Aquarium Care of Livebearers

TED DENGLER COLETTI, Ph.D.

Aquarium Care of Livebearers

Project Team
Editors: Craig Sernotti, David E. Boruchowitz
Indexer: Joann Woy
Interior Design: Leah Lococo Ltd. and Stephanie Krautheim
Design Layout: Stephanie Krautheim

T.F.H. Publications
President/CEO: Glen S. Axelrod
Executive Vice President: Mark E. Johnson
Publisher: Christopher T. Reggio
Production Manager: Kathy Bontz

T.F.H. Publications, Inc.
One TFH Plaza
Third and Union Avenues
Neptune City, NJ 07753

Discovery Communications, Inc. Book Development Team
Marjorie Kaplan, President and General Manager,
Animal Planet Media
Patrick Gates, President, Discovery Commerce
Elizabeth Bakacs, Vice President, Creative and Merchandising
Sue Perez-Jackson, Director, Licensing
Bridget Stoyko, Designer
Caitlin Erb, Licensing Manager

 Exterior design ©2008 Discovery Communications, LLC. Animal Planet, and related logos are trademarks of Discovery Communications, LLC, used under license. All rights reserved. *animalplanet.com*

Interior design, text, and photos ©2008 T.F.H. Publications, Inc.

08 09 10 11 12 1 3 5 7 9 8 6 4 2
Printed and bound in China

Library of Congress Cataloging-in-Publication Data
Coletti, Ted Dengler.
  Aquarium care of livebearers / Ted Dengler Coletti.
     p. cm. – (Animal planet pet care library)
  Includes index.
  ISBN 978-0-7938-3701-4 (alk. paper)
  1. Livebearing aquarium fishes. I. Title.
  SF458.L58C65 2008
  639.34–dc22

                          2008003243

The Leader in Responsible Animal Care for Over 50 Years!®
www.tfh.com

Table of Contents

Introduction

Take a moment and think back to your first aquarium. There is a good chance that you had some livebearing fish in that tank. Platies, swordtails, mollies, or guppies, I would guess. These fish are extraordinary in that they give birth to living young right before your eyes. The only effort on your part is to acquire a pregnant female (which is nearly always the case). Discovering fry in one's fish tank is the catalyst that turns many an aquarium owner into a more serious hobbyist. It is an experience that never really gets old, regardless of one's tenure as an aquarist.

This book was designed to fill a long overdue need in the aquarium hobby, where dated and often inaccurate information persists. It also serves to confront the misconception that livebearers are not a challenging or diverse group of fish. More than any other fish, livebearers offer something for everyone. That includes the artist, scientist, conservationist, entrepreneur, and competitor alike.

Livebearing fish are a diverse and fascinating group of aquarium fishes. Their charms and challenges await you within.

Chapter 1

A New Look at
Livebearers

No fish have made a bigger splash in the history of the tropical fish hobby than the livebearers. Today over one-third of the fish sold by Florida fish farmers are varieties of livebearers. And that's out of thousands of species and varieties of tropical fish available to hobbyists throughout the year!

It is easy to see why livebearing fish are so popular. Most of them are small, hardy, colorful, and peaceful, and they provide the wonder of live birth right in your aquarium. But livebearers are much more than just good community tank fish. Indeed, many are not well-suited to community tank life at all. But all are interesting and satisfying to work with in their own right.

What Exactly is a Livebearer?

There is no single order or family of fish that houses "the livebearers." Livebearing fish are defined by their function, not by a shared evolutionary history or taxonomy. This makes the category different from that of other popular fish groups, such as cichlids, barbs, and tetras, which all seem to share a common ancestry—although it is assumed that livebearing fish within a given family also share a common ancestry.

The livebearer category is also hard to define with commonalities. For example, some female fish, such as among the popular East African cichlids, hold their externally fertilized eggs in their mouths for protection until hatching and then release fully developed free-swimming young. Male seahorses pouch their mates' eggs for similar reasons. The hobby and scientific communities do not consider these animals livebearing fish, although if taken literally this term would be correct.

We will define a livebearer as a fish possessing three distinct traits:

- internal fertilization by the male of female eggs in utero
- internal fetal development
- live birth of independent fry

Known as vivipary, the livebearing method of reproduction functions to protect fertilized eggs from predators as well as to create larger and more well-developed fry. Viviparous

The Uncommon Adaptation

Just think for a moment what a monumental leap in evolution it is to go from laying and fertilizing eggs in the open water and having them hatch as tiny helpless fry amid numerous predators, to vivipary (internal fertilization and gestation to live birth).

As the dominant species on the planet, we tend to take livebearing for granted. But in fishdom this is a relatively uncommon adaptation. Did you know that among the estimated 28,000 identified species of fish, only about 3 percent are livebearers? Take out the ancient lineage of sharks and rays (cartilaginous fish) and the percentage of livebearing species drops to less than 2 percent of the remaining bony fish.

A *wild swordtail* Xiphophorus hellerii *collected in Belize.*

reproduction takes two forms in livebearing fish.

Truly viviparous livebearers, the first form, provide continuous nourishment and gas exchange to the developing fetuses through mechanisms connected to the mother fish's blood supply. This is similar to development with a placenta in mammals. Maternal connection can occur via a belly sac, such as in the four-eyed fish *Anableps*, or via umbilical cord-like structures, such as employed by goodeids. True vivipary results in fewer, but larger, fully formed fry than would result from the hatched eggs of an egglaying fish of comparable size; newly released livebearer fry surprise even the most seasoned hobbyist lucky enough to witness their birth.

Ovoviviparous livebearers, the second form, are essentially egglaying fish, only they are fertilizing their eggs inside the bodies of the females (called ovovivipary), instead of outside in the water (ovipary) like most other fish. Nourishment for the embryo is via the yolk sac of the egg, with some gas exchange via the womb. Most livebearers of the family Poeciliidae were long thought to use this method of reproduction, but in recent decades supplementary maternal nourishment and/or gas exchange via a quasi-placenta membrane has been discovered in many species in the genera *Poeciliopsis, Poecilia, Heterandria*, and *Xiphophorus*. Therefore the line between true vivipary and ovovivipary is blurring.

Livebearers for the aquarium hobby also come in two basic flavors: fancy and wild-type.

Fancy livebearers are generally the kind found in pet shops and fish shows. These are fish that have either been selectively cultivated over many generations or hybridized with other species or geographic races. The resulting fish have colors and finnage more elaborate and striking than those found in nature (where such a fish would be an easy target for a predator). Platies, swordtails, mollies, variatus platies, and guppies have all been fancified through the efforts of dedicated hobbyist breeders since the 1920s.

In pet shops and online auction sites, fancy livebearers are often given labels with both their common and scientific name, such as red tuxedo swordtail, *Xiphophorus hellerii*. In actuality such fish are usually hybrids of several species and races. More taxonomically attuned sellers would label them as "*Xiphophorus* sp." to indicate an unknown or mixed origin. The ethical hobbyist should do the same to ensure against false information as well as contamination of pure populations, many of which are in danger of extinction.

Wild-type livebearers are descendants of wild specimens that were collected in nature and have not been selectively bred for color, size, or finnage. These fish behave and look more like their wild ancestors. However, many of these wild-type fish have been bred for so many generations that they, too, have become domesticated to a degree, so certain desirable traits sometimes become standard within their stock. An example would be *Girardinus metallicus*, whose unique black-

SMALL FRY

So Many Fish!

Kids will have a great time running from one tank to another at your local fish or pet store to see all the available livebearers. There is a huge selection of these fish for you to choose from, from mollies to guppies to swordtails to platies to... it keeps going on and on!

throated form is distributed throughout the hobby, even though this is only one form of the species found in its native Cuba.

Domestication of wild stocks is not always a bad thing. If a large enough gene pool is utilized, successive generations tend to be hardier and adapt to aquarium conditions and dry foods much easier than their wild brethren. A good example of this is the red-tailed goodeid, *Xenotoca eiseni*, which in its aquarium-bred form is such a hardy charge that it is difficult to believe at one time it was a more delicate fish from the Mexican highlands. The hobbyist should be aware of this when considering a purchase of pure wild stock. The purchase of later generations raised in aquariums better guarantees success.

The Joy of Keeping Livebearers

Livebearers suffer from an ill-deserved reputation as bread and butter fish or fish for beginners only. In reality, nothing could be further from the truth. The combined membership of the two national livebearer hobbyist organizations in the United States exceeds that of any one of the popular cichlid, killifish, catfish, or goldfish societies. As a board member of the American Livebearer Association (ALA), I can tell you that at the time of this writing membership in the ALA has reached record levels, and Internet forums and e-mail groups dedicated just to livebearers are numerous, with new ones continuing to appear. What is going on here? The reality is that no other group of fish offers more ways to enjoy one's hobby than the livebearers.

The Wonder of Live Birth

In the previous section we discussed the various fascinating ways livebearing fish develop embryonically. In Chapter 7 we will outline the various methods of internal fertilization employed by each livebearer family. But the most thrilling aspect of the livebearing mechanism is witnessing the birth process itself. You would be hard pressed to find a veteran aquarist who doesn't remember the first time they discovered living baby fish in

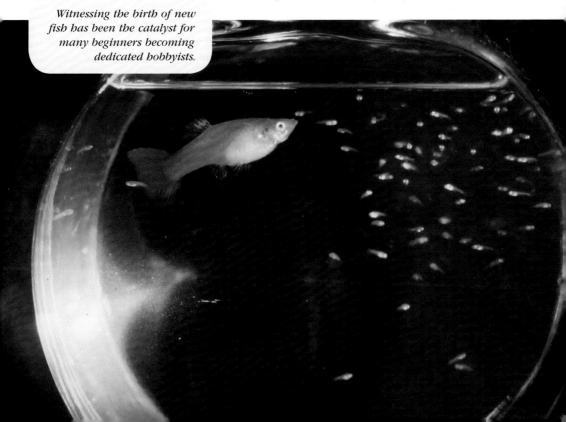

Witnessing the birth of new fish has been the catalyst for many beginners becoming dedicated hobbyists.

The pike livebearer
Belonesox belizanus *is best kept as a single specimen, as it will eat other fish.*

their aquarium. Every hobbyist should pull up a chair and try to observe a livebearing fish giving birth at least once in their hobby life. For most of us, this was the start of a lifelong hobby.

Hundreds of Species, Thousands of Varieties

Pet shop guppies, platies, swordtails, and mollies just scratch the surface. There are over 300 species of aquarium-suitable freshwater livebearers residing in over 70 genera, in four families across two orders of fishes. And that does not even include all the distinct geographic populations and fancy varieties! More species and varieties enter the scientific or hobby community every year. When you take

all this into account, the number of aquarium livebearers today is easily in the thousands.

Challenging Charges

Many livebearers are hardy fish that will adjust to most water conditions and breed quite readily. Their fry are hardy, and if separated from their parents—who will often eat their young—survival is just about ensured. Most are peaceful.

But many livebearers require skill and dedication on the part of the hobbyist. This could be because of dietary requirements, special water and temperature conditions, tank setup, wild-caught status, or aggressive tendencies. An example of a challenging and labor-intensive livebearer is Central America's *Belonesox belizanus*, the pike livebearer. Hailing from the same family as the peaceful guppy, this fish is an ambush predator. In fact, it eats peaceful guppies. Females have been known to make a meal of their mates, too. Fry and juveniles must be protected from their parents and usually fed tiny live foods to ensure good growth and health.

Some livebearers possess genetics that make the development of fancy forms particularly challenging. Take the humble and peaceful platy, *Xiphophorus maculatus*. In most platies, sex is determined as in mammals, by X and Y chromosomes, with XX being female and XY being male. Some strains of platies, however, possess two of three sex chromosomes (X, Y, and W), which results in two kinds of males (XY and YY) and three kinds of females (XX, WX, and WY). Since color and fin traits are often linked to the Y chromosome, this makes selective breeding for certain traits and new fancy varieties very interesting and challenging.

Courtship and Mating Rituals

Many livebearers display complex mating behavior. Rituals may include males making a territory to wait for females, displaying elaborate or erect finnage, and even discharging chemical signals in their urine. Females of these species will show a preferences for certain colors, finnage, pheromones, or body size that has important consequences for the evolution of their species.

Complex Social Behavior

Each livebearer species exhibits a unique temperament, social structure, and feeding style for you the home aquarist to observe and enjoy. The competition for mates and food, as well as the cycle of birth (which can be seasonal in some species, namely goodeids), creates an interesting social milieu in livebearer colonies. This behavior changes as the fish mature from fry to juveniles to adults.

A common social expression in livebearing fish is the emergence of the alpha male, a more aggressive, larger, or more colorful fish that dominates the colony until the fish in it fall into a pecking order. Schooling behavior may also be observed in some species, especially among juveniles. If you breed livebearers just as part of a breeder award program in your local fish club, and then quickly discard them, you are missing out on some great observational experiences as they grow and develop. Real fans not only breed their fish but also try to understand them.

Fun with Genetics

Because livebearers give birth so regularly (every 24 to 65 days at peak

The Leap Fish Phenomenon

...ebearer breeders often notice that one fish seems to grow faster and emerge as a ...e before the others in its brood. Sometimes this is the most aggressive sibling. As ...ecomes an adult, it often emerges as the top fish in the pecking order. Swordtails ... variatus platies are notorious for this development.

This fish is known as the alpha male, and it generally cannot tolerate other males ...ts tank. The growth rate of the other fish now slows (but at a normal growth rate). ...obyists and breeders often jump to the erroneous conclusion (and worry) that they ...e only one male to work with in an entire brood, with the rest a tank full of ...dersized females.

But then something interesting happens. Another fish eventually grows ... size exceeding that of the alpha male, and then (very suddenly) takes ...the physical characteristics of a male! A battle ensues, with the larger fish ...oming (or remaining) the alpha male.

Discovered in the early 1970s, this strange activity was termed the "leap fish ...nomenon." Male livebearers will literally "stealth" themselves as females to avoid ...ng bullied or killed by the present alpha male or adult fish. I have observed young ...e variatus platies even taking on the gravid spot and full abdomen of a female ...urvive.

The implication to breeders is obvious: be patient. There are more males than you ...nk, and the larger males will emerge in time. It is the misunderstanding of this ...nomenon that probably resulted in the undersized swordtails in today's pet shop ...ins. By continually removing the largest males from farm ponds for retail over ... years, fish farmers have essentially been using the smaller and smaller males as ...eding stock—worsening the problem with every harvesting.

Here a male Xiphophorus variatus *swims with a female… or another male in disguise. This is an example of the leap fish adaptation.*

also the scientific community. Many of the resulting offspring had full black finnage everywhere, as well as a little black "mustache" mark on the lips. Apparently a gene that moderates the comet pattern or other black pigmentation was not inherited in some of the offspring.

What this means to you as the hobbyist is that when playing with livebearer genetics you may encounter some unexpected but very rewarding surprises.

season, depending on species) the hobbyist is presented with a handy living model to study dominant and recessive traits with great efficiency. You can create your own living genetics experiments by crossing various fish having certain physical characteristics to see which traits (and genes) are dominant or recessive. With many livebearers, especially those in the *Xiphophorus* genus (platies and swordtails), this often leads to unexpected results as new gene combinations create new color patterns, sex ratios, body shapes, and finnage. And this is where the fun begins!

Take for example a staple of the aquarium hobby, the wagtail platy. Dr. Myron Gordon, a famed geneticist, attempted a seemingly simple cross in his New York City fish laboratory in the early 1930s. A wild gray *X. maculatus* platy with a comet-tail pattern (two stripes nearly forming two sides of a triangle) was crossed with the recently developed hobby-strain gold platy. The results astounded not only Gordon but

Creating Your Own Strain

Both amateur and professional breeders are developing and improving upon fancy livebearer strains all the time by selectively inbreeding and crossing their fish. Why not you?

Serendipity has been the source for most of the major fancy strains on the market today. In the March 1961 issue of *Tropical Fish Hobbyist*, the world was introduced to Mrs. Thelma Hobson Simpson of Gardena, California, who discovered the "hifin" trait as a sport in one of her swordtail tanks. Selectively breeding her fish over several generations created swordtails with larger and fuller hifins (larger dorsal fins, the fin on the fish's back). Later, hobbyists in Hawai'i and Florida crossed her swordtails with platies and variatus platies to create wonderful new fish for the hobby.

There are many livebearers that are facing complete extinction. This Skiffia francesae, *for example, no longer exists in the wild, and is surviving only because of the aquarium hobby and in public aquariums.*

Similar breeding surprises could be had with forced hybridization of different color or finnage strains. The platies, swords, and mollies that grace your pet shop are nearly all hybrids created over the last 80 years by dedicated breeders for our enjoyment. Many possibilities still await the hobbyist willing to attempt new crosses—and be responsible enough to label them as such so as not to contaminate pure species. Several hobbyists make a nice side income, or at least partially fund their hobby, selling their home-bred fish over the Internet or to pet shops.

Species Maintenance and Conservation

A sad fact of the livebearer hobby is that many of our species have become poster children for the conservation and biodiversity movements. *Skiffia francesae, Xiphophorus couchianus,* and *Zoogoneticus tequila* are already extinct in nature and holding on only in public aquariums and hobbyist fishrooms.

Others were less lucky. *Gambusia amistadensis,* saved from extinction in 1968, died out even in captivity in 1984. Many more livebearers become endangered as the bodies of water they inhabit dry up, become polluted, or get infested with introduced game species. The biodiversity of livebearers is shrinking at a remarkable rate. Setting up a 10- or 20-gallon (40- or 80-liter) species maintenance tank for an endangered species is a very commendable reason—maybe even the best reason—to keep a livebearer.

Competitive Showing

Just as we have dog shows with judges, standards, classes, and award levels, there are also fish shows.

Some livebearer shows, like the ones sanctioned by the International Fancy Guppy Association, are professionally organized with highly trained judges. Breeding and raising a fish for a show requires a somewhat different level of dedication on the part of the hobbyist, but the feeling of accomplishment when one's fish takes home a trophy makes it all worthwhile.

Fishy Fellowship

The livebearer hobby has a vast social network attached to it. Each year livebearer shows and weekend conventions are held in different parts of the country, often with guest speakers. There are local livebearer clubs in some major metropolitan areas that meet regularly too. Internet blogs and message forums dedicated to livebearers are numerous. All these activities offer the chance to make new friends with those who share your interests, and to exchange ideas and livestock. The auctions and trading posts associated with these groups are where many hobbyists acquire the rare livebearers they cannot find anywhere else.

Ready, Set, Go!

Suffice it to say that there is no specialty within the aquarium hobby that appeals to such a diversity of interests as livebearing fish. Whether you consider yourself an introvert or extrovert, artist or scientist, entrepreneur or naturalist, conservationist or competitor, your interests will find refuge within one or more aspects of the livebearer hobby.

Ready to take the plunge into the livebearer world? Not so fast. Next we need to discuss how to successfully maintain the livebearer aquarium without wasting your time or money.

Chapter 2

Water Quality, the Secret to a
No-Fail Aquarium

Fishkeeping is easier now than at any other time in history. Reliable and affordable equipment, quality fish food, and scientific knowledge that has expunged many an old myth has resulted in today's home aquariums being a reliable and low maintenance addition to your life. Unfortunately, the conventional wisdom still is that aquariums are messy, laborious, and susceptible to sick fish. These next few chapters will dispel those myths and point you in the right direction to success.

While aquarium equipment and methods have evolved, the same cannot be said for good advice. Mass retailing has resulted in more poorly trained staff providing erroneous information. Older books from a library (personal or public) are often outdated. So before we embark on the wonderful world of livebearers and the supplies you will require, let's review the information you need to ensure your success working with them.

The most important thing you can do to keep your fish healthy and your aquarium sweet-smelling is to properly maintain the water quality. Regular partial water changes, the right filtration, and light feedings are the secrets that successful fish keepers have mastered. But there are right and wrong ways to do these things, and more often than not, the new hobbyist is advised of or practices the wrong methods.

Biological Filtration

The reason why fish can live happily in an aquarium, when in reality they are literally swimming in their own toilet, is because otherwise harmful waste products are being consumed by other aquarium dwellers or converted into or locked up in less harmful substances by chemical reactions in the aquarium.

The most important diners at this feast are bacteria. *Good* bacteria. Aerobic (oxygen-consuming) bacteria to be specific. During the six to eight weeks after the start of a new aquarium, aerobic bacteria grow large colonies in an aquarium. All will eventually reside on the surfaces in your tank, but the most concentrated colony will be in your filter. The media for this bacterial bed can be sponges, plastic webbing, ceramic noodles, plastic balls, or revolving pleated fabric wheels.

One group of aerobic bacteria converts ammonia, released by the fish through their respiration and waste elimination and also by the decomposition of organic substances in the aquarium, to nitrite, while another group converts this nitrite to nitrate. Nitrate is relatively harmless to fish at low levels, but it can be used as a food source for the growth of unsightly algae. At high levels it can lower disease resistance and affect the growth of your fry. Regular water changes and the use of live plants reduce all forms of nitrogenous waste, including nitrates.

The key point here is that it takes time to develop an adequate colony of aerobic bacteria to biologically filter

Cycling Your Tank Faster

There are ways to speed up the six-week process needed to fully colonize a biological filter. Besides using live plants to take up nitrogenous wastes, you can also jump start your new tank's bacteria bed by seeding it with a little gravel from a healthy established aquarium.

Java fern and Java moss will provide excellent vegetative filtration and a home for newborn fry.

your aquarium. The hobbyist should start with only one or two very small, hardy fish to cycle a new aquarium for the first two months. Platies are an excellent choice for this. Alternatively, you can heavily plant the aquarium from the start, as plants also consume ammonia products.

Many new hobbyists make the mistake—indeed are even advised sometimes by pet store staff—to discard and change the biological component of their filter on a regular basis. Doing this, especially in the absence of live plants, can result in dangerous ammonia spikes and may be a cause for why so many new hobbyists fail. Similarly, cleaning biological media under chlorinated tap water can kill a large part of this good bacteria bed too. Biological media should be gently rinsed in the water you remove from your aquarium at water changes.

Vegetative Filtration

The most comprehensive and underutilized form of filtration in today's aquarium hobby is vegetative filtration. But this type of filtration is a vital component of water quality in the wild and was the primary source of filtration for the aquarium hobby for its first 100 years.

Prior to the 1950s, plants provided the primary filtration for aquariums (although at the time this true benefit was not fully realized). Plant use for this purpose then declined in the U.S. over the remainder of the century to almost a strictly ornamental value. Unsuitable house and bog plants were often (and still are) sold to hobbyists. All this changed in the 1990s when European and Japanese methods brought true aquatic plants back into stores and hobbyists' hearts.

The Best Plants for Vegetative Fitration in a Livebearer Tank

- Java fern, *Microsorum pteropus,* and Java moss, *Taxiphyllum barbieri*: Grows best along wood, porous rocks, and on top of gravel. Never bury its rhizome (horizontal stem that sends out roots)! Tolerates low light.

- Spiral val, *Vallisneria spiralis*: Rooted plant that can get its carbon from minerals in the water. Needs moderate to bright light. Shallow roots. Reproduces by runner plants. Needs established or fertilized gravel bed to thrive.

- Tropical hornwort, *Ceratophyllum submersum*: Rootless, it floats or can be held down by a stone or ornament. Can get its carbon from minerals in the water.

- *Cryptocoryne wendtii*: A low-light rooted plant, it grows best and is more effective in groups. Stays low.

- *Hygrophila polysperma*: Rooted plant with delicate stems that creates a bushy effect when pruned. Tolerates moderate light well. Banned in many states because it can overwinter in natural waters, it is available as sunset hygro in some shops or through aquarium clubs.

Hygrophila polysperma

Microsorum pteropus

Cryptocoryne wendtii "bronze"

Vallisneria spiralis

Plants in an aquarium, as in nature, remove nitrogenous wastes excreted by fish and decaying food and plant matter. Besides consuming ammonia, nitrite, and nitrate, plants also metabolize phosphates and some metals, traces of which can be found in tap water and flake food. Aquarium plants also require carbon dioxide (CO_2) and light to perform photosynthesis (the creation of sugars), both of which are plentiful above the water (and why many nurseries grow their plants emersed, poking out of the stock pool). The carbonic acids produced by decaying food, wood, fish wastes, and respiration also are a source of CO_2.

Therefore the best plants for most livebearer tanks are ones that thrive in lower light (and thus need less CO_2), or can float on the surface to receive more of both. Plants that tolerate the harder water that most livebearers enjoy and also need little or no gravel (leaf feeders rather than root feeders) are also preferred for the livebearer aquarium.

Chemical Filtration

Over time, end products from the metabolism of wastes, the natural decay of food, wood, and old plants, and fish emissions such as pheromones, slime coats, etc., build up in an aquarium beyond what aerobic bacteria and aquarium plants can neutralize, or metabolize to waste products that cannot be utilized efficiently. These waste products are called dissolved organic compounds (DOCs). DOCs can tint and acidify your aquarium water and create a stale smell. As they build up, they can lower the immunity and growth rate of your livebearers.

This is where adsorptive media like activated carbon prove helpful. Most filters contain activated carbon either as a granular add-in or as impregnated within the filter medium itself. While the amount of activated carbon in aquarium filters is far too little to have any long-lasting effect, its periodic use when you need to change the filter medium will provide some extra polishing of your water that will help maintain good quality. It also will remove medications from the water when a treatment regimen is complete. Using chemical filtration, though, is not an excuse for avoiding water changes, overfeeding, or using other forms of filtration.

Don't Overfeed

Overfeeding is often cited as the primary hobbyist behavior that kills or sickens fish. Overfeeding creates more nitrogenous wastes and DOCs than the growing bacteria bed and live plants can consume.

This does not mean, however, that you should skip a feeding (another old fishwives' tale that can allow internal parasites a chance to dig in, literally).

Feeding multiple times a day is best, but if you can feed only once a day, make sure all your fish get to eat. Just feed very lightly without wasting any food. My tip: think of a fish's stomach as about as big as its eye, and then feed accordingly.

What you feed your fish is important too. Fortunately, most of today's commercial fish foods provide a complete diet and a variety of live and prepared foods is readily available. We'll talk in more detail about choosing and storing the right food for your livebearers in Chapter 4.

Water Changes...Water Changes...Water Changes!

Although biological, vegetative, and chemical filtration, combined with appropriate feeding, solves most of the problem with maintaining an aquarium, over the long run DOCs can still build up in an aquarium, as can bad bacteria, free-swimming pathogens, fungi, etc. Aquarium water will eventually acidify and lose some of its buffering (carbonate hardness, or KH) capacity. Even in an efficiently functioning aquarium, the water will not be as fresh as can be found in most wild sources.

This is where water changes come in. In your parents' (or maybe your grandparents') day, "old water" was prized, and water was simply topped off (water lost to evaporation was replaced with new fresh water). Aquarists got away with this bad practice because the species sold at the time were generally small and could take a lot of abuse. Tanks were heavily planted, providing key vegetative filtration. But this practice also resulted in many decimated new aquariums, as ammonia and nitrites built up in the first two months before an aerobic bacteria bed could be established.

Ask any veteran aquarist of today what is the single best thing you can do for your aquarium and they will probably tell you, "Water changes." Many of us notice an obvious perking up of our fish after a partial water change. Breeders swear by them for conditioning their fish to spawn. Better resistance to and recovery from disease is a well-known anecdotal observation. And in the first two months of an aquarium's life, regular water changes are critical to keep ammonia and nitrite under control until your biological filter becomes fully functioning.

SMALL FRY

How to Feed Your Fish

Young children may think they are helping their small water friends by giving them lots of food several times a day, but this is more harmful than helpful. Offered portions should be small and monitored closely by an adult.

Regular water changes will keep your fish healthy and happy.

Contrary to popular belief, water changes do not have to be laborious. They can be as simple as placing a rinsed plastic pitcher (dedicated only to aquarium use) into the aquarium to remove water and replace it with fresh, conditioned tap water. You need not remove the fish and strip down the tank during a water change. Indeed this will result in more harm than good, as you disturb the beneficial bacterial colonies and stress your animals. There are even siphon hoses that hook up to your faucet these days that allow you to drain and fill a tank while simultaneously vacuuming the gravel bed, without ever having to carry a bucket! (More on this in the next chapter.) The more often you change your water the better; the more water you change the better.

When adding fresh water to an aquarium, two precautions should be employed. First, it is important to run your tap for 30 seconds to a minute to remove any residual copper from the water that might have leached from your indoor pipes. Copper is highly toxic to fish, and long-term exposure can lead to illness and death. Secondly, make sure the new water is the same temperature as that in the aquarium. Adding a dash of heated water to your bucket usually does the trick.

Either way, water changes make a *huge* impact on the health of your fish and appearance of your aquarium.

Off to the Store

Now that you know the secrets leading to a no-fail livebearer aquarium, let's go shopping for the right gear to make it happen—and learn what to avoid!

Chapter 3

Getting the

Right Gear

With the plethora of products on the market today, many of which you do not need or should not buy, purchasing an aquarium setup can be a vexing undertaking. There is no FDA for fish food. No Consumer Protection Agency for aquarium products. Nearly anything can be marketed as essential, healthy, or handy. Unfamiliar imported brands, many cheap but unreliable, are now flooding the market. So let's cut through all the hype and talk the *right* gear.

Tank and Stand

There is literally a livebearer for any size of aquarium. The diminutive *Heterandria formosa* can form a colony in a 2-gallon (8-liter) tank, and a pair of guppies or platies can do well in many of the various desktop aquariums. Chapter 7 provides guidelines for minimum tank sizes, but the old adage of "get the biggest aquarium you can fit and afford" still holds true.

Larger aquariums are more stable in terms of temperature. They have more room for territories and hiding places. They are less likely to become overstocked, resulting in better water quality. They are generally easier to clean. All-glass aquariums manufactured by established companies are your best choice. Acrylic tanks, mostly seen in mini desktop aquaria, are particularly sturdy and good for children. But they also show scratches more easily.

Many livebearers are proficient jumpers, so a tank cover with openings only for filters and heaters is highly recommended. A solid cover also keeps out unwanted debris and keeps in desired and expensive heat.

A sturdy stand for your aquarium is a must. I prefer solid wood or iron stands rather than pressboard, as these tend be the strongest and resist soaking up water. You can buy most aquariums in combination with an appropriate stand.

Aquascaping Materials

The twenty-first century offers the most realistic plastic plants, wood, ornaments, and rockwork ever available, making it easy to create just about any underwater design that suits your imagination. I now prefer artificial wood to real, as it does not promote the buildup of DOCs (dissolved organic carbons) that add to the bioload and smell of an aquarium. They also sink

Shown here is a swordtail with elongated finnage. Make sure your tank and stand are level.

naturally. My tip: drill some small holes in the back, bottom, and top of artificial wood and rocks to allow better water circulation inside the ornament.

Small rocks are always a nice choice for an aquarium, and the ones you find in your back yard will do just fine. Give them a good scrubbing with a stiff brush and some salt and baking soda to remove any dirt or herbicide and pesticide residue. A wonderful rock for most livebearer tanks is the tufa or lava rocks sold in natural beige-white and red-brown. These are calcareous, so they help simulate the natural calcium-hard and alkaline water that most livebearers enjoy or tolerate well.

Be careful about placing too many heavy rocks in an all-glass aquarium. And when positioning a rock, never drop it down into the tank, but place it gently on the bottom. My tip: use aquarium silicone sealant to hold rocks of various sizes together.

Gravel is usually used to excess in the aquarium. A deep gravel bed, with no circulation, can become a breeding ground for unwanted bacteria, noxious wastes, and parasites. It is often hard to clean. If not using rooted plants, it is best to only apply a sprinkling of gravel to just cover the bottom glass, and employ a gravel siphon when changing water.

Filters

There is a dizzying array of aquarium filters on the market, with new models and brands coming and going all the time. Go with an established, time-tested brand and model. It has proved

its staying power, and replacement parts and media will always be available. When pricing a filter, compare the costs of the replacement media as well as the unit itself. Sometimes that inexpensive or cutting-edge filter will cost you more in the long run.

Power filters offer the best combination of convenience, reliability, and versatility for the hobbyist. Most hang on the outside of the aquarium and are easiest to service and tend to filter better. Others can be placed inside the tank, which is good when you need your aquarium flush against a wall or want something quieter. Unknown to most hobbyists, internal power filters also provide some heat, which will save on heater operation costs.

A thermometer is an important piece of equipment for your aquarium.

millennium. Make sure your heater is UL (Underwriter Laboratories) tested and from a company with the experience and reputation in making quality heaters. An experienced aquarist or aquarium blog can advise on the best brands.

A thermometer will be needed to set your heater to the right setting and to monitor temperature. Check it every day if you can to ensure your heater is working properly and your fish are not being chilled

A good power filter should have separate media for biological, mechanical, and chemical filtration. And, while we are talking about filtration, we remind you again: don't forget the plants!

Heat

Most of our available livebearers, being of Central American or even North American origin, withstand lower temperatures than other tropical fish. (Chapter 7 can advise on temperature requirements per species.) But a quality heater is still necessary. Don't skimp here. There has been a flood of cheaply made imported heaters entering the market in the new

Are Blue Fish Really Blue?

Many freshwater fish photos are notorious in over-emphasizing blue and green iridescence. But blues and greens are *not* color pigments in fish skin—they result from light refraction caused by iridiophores: colorless pigment cells that reflect light. As an example, if you took a bluejay or peacock feather and cracked it with a hammer, it would appear gray, as the iridiophores and structure of the feathers that created the blue have been destroyed.

(which lowers disease resistance) or overheated (which can overtax their metabolism and shorten their lifespan).

Light

The aquarium industry has at last entered the modern age with efficient tank lighting. Gone are the days of heavy ballasts that run hot, replaceable starters, and incandescent bulbs. Make sure your fixture is fluorescent, which will cost less in the long run. Also, make sure it has an electronic starter and ballast, which will save on electricity, extend your bulb life, and run cooler. This is an environment-friendly choice too.

The fluorescent bulbs that come with aquarium strip lights are wonderful for bringing out the reds and blues in your fish. They also are adequate for growing low-light plants. My tip: when you need a replacement, the inexpensive "plant and aquarium" bulbs sold in the hardware sections of most stores are the most cost effective.

If you plan to keep a wider variety of live plants, the best bulb is one that comes closest to natural sunlight. Known as full spectrums, these bulbs usually have names like "sunshine" and "chroma" in their brand names and are available in the hardware sections of most stores at affordable prices. They emit a whiter light. Ironically, daylight-type bulbs are actually not full spectrum, but they do come closer than the standard "cool white" bulbs with their old-fashioned yellow-green casts.

Livebearers, like most other tropical fish, do well with a 12-hour cycle of daylight. If you cannot reliably turn on and off your aquarium lights every 10 to 14 hours, your best bet would be to purchase a simple timer, as well as a power strip for the heater, filter, and light strip. Aquarium and reptile power strips are now available that contain both a timer and additional plugs in one unit.

GF(C)I

The most overlooked piece of aquarium gear is the ground fault circuit interrupter, or GF(C)I, which shuts off the

A GF(C)I outlet is a must when dealing with water. Water and electricity don't mix, and this type of outlet will prevent serious harm to you if the two should ever meet.

How Much Does an Aquarium Weigh?

A filled and equipped fish tank weighs about 10 pounds per gallon. So a typical 20-gallon glass aquarium, with rocks, gravel, and ornaments, weighs approximately 200 pounds. Never try to lift a full aquarium. Besides the potential for serious injury, the weight may pop out one of the glass panes or cause the entire thing to slip out of your hands.

flow of free electricity before it can deliver a dangerous shock. These devices can easily be installed into your existing outlet by an adult who follows the package directions carefully. You can also hire an electrician to install one, or purchase a plug-in GF(C)I outlet at a hardware store. Only one-tenth of an ampere of free electricity can kill a person with water as a conductor. This simple precaution cannot be underscored enough! All GF(C)Is come with a tester button, so you can always know whether your outlet is functioning properly or not.

Other Equipment

For water changes you will need a conditioner that neutralizes chlorine, chloramines, and heavy metals. You will also need a *new* bucket dedicated only to aquarium use. For removing water, a dedicated plastic pitcher works fine, but a siphon tube with a bulb starter and gravel vacuum head makes life easier. My tip: purchase a siphon with soft tubing, which doesn't kink and is more flexible.

A wonderful product marketed by several companies is the all-in-one water changer/gravel vacuum. These devices hook up to your faucet and can siphon, vacuum, and fill your tank without you ever having to carry buckets of water back and forth.

A definite time and burden saver, though to create suction they produce considerable waste water. My tip, if you decide to use such a device: once the siphon has started, try shutting off the faucet and seeing whether the siphon action continues. It should, albeit slower. This is better for our environment.

An optional accessory is an air pump. The power filter will provide plenty of aeration, so unless you have a fishroom with multiple tanks with box or sponge filters, the use of an air pump is strictly for ornamental reasons. Many hobbyists enjoy the bubble makers and colorful moving ornaments that are available for aquariums. In this case, purchase a small but high-quality established brand of pump and make sure the bubbles created are gentle enough for your fish. Purchase a check valve so that during a power outage water does not siphon back into your pump and damage it. My tip: place your air pump on an old mouse pad or piece of rigid foam board to lessen its noise.

Lastly, a net is necessary for introducing new fish and removing others. Try to avoid the cheaper hard-mesh nets. Nets of a softer, tighter weave are easier on the delicate slime coat and scales of many fish. They are worth the extra money.

SMALL FRY

Only the Best

You want the best for your children, so teach them that only the best will do for their fish. However, finding the best materials for your fish does not mean going out and buying the most expensive gear. Careful research—most of which can be done on the Internet or by talking to veteran hobbyists or trustworthy vendors—will teach you and your kids what's best for your fish.

Chapter 4

Eating Well

There is probably nothing more confusing for hobbyists than fish food. Flakes, pellets, crisps, crumbles, sticks, frozen, canned, freeze-dried, live—the choices are endless in both the variety and confusion they bring. Big multi-national corporations to small fishroom guys manufacture and sell the stuff. Common marketing themes include "technologically advanced," "trusted brand," "miracle," and "fishroom-tested." Endorsements from a hobby star or research lab also are common.

This is not to say that the available fish foods are inadequate or that the folks who invent them are not passionate about what they do. The hobbyist today is afforded a better selection of quality fish foods than at any other time in the history of the hobby. It is just the decision about what to buy and how much to spend that is so daunting. So what should you use?

This is not an easy question, as it depends on another question: what's your goal? Is it fast growth or long life? Big body or better color? Good health or inducement to spawning? An experienced breeder can tell you that no one food does all these things. For example, a high protein content (over 45 percent) is good for growth, but a lower number is generally better for a fish's kidneys, liver, and longevity. The goal for my collection of livebearers is optimal health and a natural, if not extended, life cycle. This is different from that of the showman/breeder who requires fast growth, large fish, and enhanced color for competition.

Whatever the goal, feeding should always be light, and should be offered at least once a day.

Why Your Choice of Food is So Important

One could argue that nothing you do as a hobbyist is more important than adequate feeding. An undernourished animal cannot maintain its health and be productive, regardless of its water quality. Fortunately, today's fish foods meet this need very adequately. But it is still important that you choose the right diet and store your food properly to maximize the health, growth, and longevity of your fish.

A varied diet will help your fish thrive.

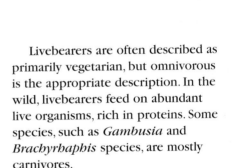

The majority of fish food research has been in relation to commercially important fish such as trout and salmon. This information is quite applicable since all fish have basically the same muscle and organ systems (from river trout to brackish mollies) and they all use the same metabolic pathways. Certain fish require other nutrients, however. Many poeciliid livebearers appreciate some vegetable matter in their diet. Surface livebearers, like halfbeaks and *Anableps*, are insectivores.

Aquarium hobbyists have needs as well in terms of fish food. We nurture our fish as pets or show animals. We want them to be colorful. We need to maintain good water quality. Plus we demand convenience.

All You Really Need to Know About Fish Food

- *The protein must be complete.*
  Protein (amino acids) is the most important component of your fish's diet. Protein intake determines growth, is used as the primary energy source, is required for tissue repair, and aids in immune response. But if the protein is not easily digestible or is missing even one key amino acid, all these things will suffer. The difficulty arises in the amount of each type of amino acid required per species. Excessive amounts can be detrimental to a particular species (e.g., spine curvature) as can a lack (e.g., stunted growth).

Livebearers are often described as primarily vegetarian, but omnivorous is the appropriate description. In the wild, livebearers feed on abundant live organisms, rich in proteins. Some species, such as *Gambusia* and *Brachyrhaphis* species, are mostly carnivores.

Algae are a part of many livebearers' diets too, and the proteins algae provide balance those found in animal matter. The popular cyanobacterium known as spirulina algae has a cell wall rich in muco-proteins that enhance the natural mucous layer of the fish's skin, as well as a special protein called phycocyanin, which may improve liver and kidney function.

Quality proteins are expensive to produce. Fish use a lot of energy to break down cheaper proteins. Fish by-products from the filleting industry (e.g., white fishmeal) have a higher level of ash and lower level

SMALL FRY

Are Sea Monkeys the Best Live Food?

Your children, or you when you were their age, may have come across an advertisement for small creatures known as sea monkeys. You sent away for them and once the package arrived and was set up you may have watched them swimming about in their container. Sea monkeys are actually brine shrimp. Brine shrimp, *Artemia* sp., are small saltwater crustaceans that can be found all over the world, including places like the Great Salt Lake in Utah, San Francisco Bay, and salt lakes in Canada, Russia, and China. In the late 1950s brine shrimp were novelty-marketed as pets in various advertising media, mostly aimed at kids, although of course they were at the same time being sold to fish hobbyists by aquarium-oriented concerns (such as the San Francisco Aquarium Society) primarily as a staple item of fish food. Newly hatched brine shrimp are a nearly perfect fish food. The hard, air-tight shell of their tiny eggs means they can be stored for years before being hatched in warm salted water.

of protein than whole fishmeals. Whole fish as an ingredient is probably better, containing the necessary amino acids in proper proportion.

- *Use fish fats.* Fats (lipids) supply fish with energy, structure, and aid in other functions. Fish get lipids from both vegetable and animal matter. As with proteins, the right kinds in the right amounts are key. This is easily provided by ingredients of marine origins, such as fish meal and fish oil, like cod liver.

- *It has to be digested to work.* More digestible food results in healthier fish and the buildup of fewer waste products in your aquarium. But the fish have to eat the food in the first place. Some fish will more readily eat one brand of food than another.

  Check the ash content of your fish food. Ash generally affects digestibility of dry matter, resulting in higher waste outputs, and can also produce mineral imbalances. For flake and freeze-dried foods, the type of drying technique used during processing is another very important factor. Flame-dried products are less digestible.

- *Keep it fresh.* Most hobbyists keep their dry fish food far too long. Fats from fish oil, while optimal, are rich in polyunsaturates and are susceptible to going rancid. Toxic compounds, such as histamine, cadaverine, and agmatine, can arise with aged or spoiled foods based on fish.

The author with his daughter and a bag of frozen paste food. Such foods may be smelly, but they are an excellent addition to your fish's diet.

As soon as ingredients leave their natural state (i.e., alive), their usefulness as a food diminishes. This is why feeding live foods works so well. Fish food ingredients should be minimally and quickly processed after harvest or capture. Good luck finding a manufacturer that will put a freshness date on your fish food. So here are some tips:

For frozen food, stock up in the winter. This helps ensure the food remains frozen. Packages should be flat and uniform. Look inside the cardboard sleeved packages to make sure the food exhibits a uniform mold. For dry foods, buy small jars and keep them in a cool dry place (ideally: refrigerated; worst: on top of the light strip). Try to use opened cans within a month. Excess food can be frozen in freezer bags until ready to use.

The Optimal Livebearer Diet

Most livebearers are small-mouthed surface or mid-water feeders—although there are many exceptions to this rule. Diets designed for guppies are

Food Facts

- **Flakes:** will float and are easy to shake out. But they also dissolve their nutrients into the water faster.
- **Pellets:** remain more solid, but sink. Buy a small size like "guppy" or "micro" for livebearers.
- **Sticks:** best for pond fish or large cichlids—not most livebearers.
- **Freeze-Dried:** brine shrimp, daphnia, tubifex worms, and mosquito larvae work well with the small mouths of most livebearers. Make sure the brand you buy is cleaned or sterilized. A vitamin-infused brand is even better.
- **Live:** most nutritious food. Daphnia, newly hatched brine shrimp, and wingless fruit flies are best for livebearers and can be cultured at home.

great for Central and South American livebearers. Flakes and floating micro-sized pellets are good dry foods. Brine shrimp, mosquito larvae, daphnia, and bloodworms are among the suitable freeze-dried choices, and most of these foods can be obtained in frozen form as well. (Hobbyists beware: the use of bloodworms, the larval form of an insect, can result in a prolonged severe hay-fever-like allergic reaction that lasts a day or more in about 10 percent of the population.)

Variety is key. Fish combine what amino acids they can into proteins within a couple of hours, and convert the remainder into energy. Studies indicate that a guppy, for example, digests a meal after about 45 minutes.

With this in mind, I recommend mixing a few different varieties of dry and freeze-dried foods to ensure a complete diet. Most livebearers also relish the soft inner flesh of blanched zucchini, cucumber, and peas crushed in your fingers over the top of the tank.

You can supplement dry foods with frozen foods. Many hobbyists create their own frozen

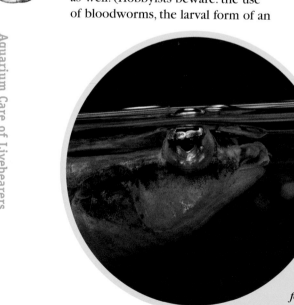

Anableps have adapted to see both above and below the water line, perfect for finding food and watching for predators at the same time.

What is the Best Food for Livebearer Breeding?

Something that all of us fishheads desire are large broods of fry from our female livebearers. In the 1970s, scientists decided to do a test with adult guppies using various foods, both as single feeds and in mixes of different foods. The results? While fresh earthworms were the single best food (followed by beef heart or tubifex, then brine shrimp), the combinations worked even better. Earthworms plus dry food, or earthworms plus beef heart plus lettuce, were associated with the most fry drops (births). Granted, the dry foods at the time were not of the quality we enjoy today. So from this study and our previous discussion, I'd bet my money on a combination of live food and homemade dry blend fed at the same time to ensure optimal health and big drops from my livebearers.

with blanched carrots, garlic, and romaine lettuce in a food processor. Add prepared gelatin (before it cools) to this mixture and let it set in the refrigerator overnight. You can then store the food in flat, thin portions in several freezer bags in your freezer and break off a small piece when needed.

But remember that you just can't beat the freshness of live foods. In the wild, livebearers feed on insects and various crustaceans in their biotope, so wingless fruit flies and brine shrimp prove very appropriate for livebearers. When you feed a live food, feed another type right after, or top off your charges with your dry food blend, to make the meal as complete as possible.

In terms of fish food, variety truly is the spice of life. Just keep it fresh and feed it lightly.

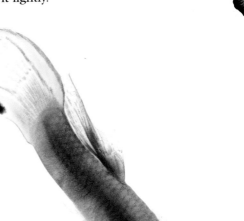

paste foods. Recipes abound, but an easy one appropriate for livebearers entails mincing ingredients like shrimp and water-packed sardines along

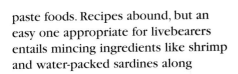

Chapter 5

Selecting Your Stock and

Keeping it Healthy

The most common complaint from *former* home aquarists is that the fish kept getting sick and dying. In reality, these folks probably received poor advice or did not heed or look for the guidance needed to create a successful aquarium.

Let's review the major points from the last three chapters of this book:

- Maintain good water quality through regular water changes, light feeding, and a diversity of filtration.

- Select the right high-quality equipment.

- Provide a diverse, nutritious diet.

If you have done these things, you are well on your way to avoiding nearly all maladies that can afflict your fish and crash your aquarium. A healthy livebearing fish can fend off or keep at bay nearly all the pathogens that commonly infect an aquarium. But there still is one more ounce of prevention that you need to master: selecting healthy fish in the first place!

An Avoidance Checklist

Your choice of fish for purchase is a critical decision. Selecting a sick or diseased fish most always leads to disappointment, death, and possible infection of the tank's other denizens. Pet shop fish require the most caution, as they have undergone the stress of shipping and may be kept in crowded conditions or with central filtration systems that spread disease across multiple tanks. Fortunately, it is fairly easy to spot most fish problems before you tell the pet store worker, "I'll take that one!"

When you see any of the following attributes in a livebearer, it is best to pass it by:

- numerous dead fish in the aquarium (contagion or acclimation problem)

- tiny white or black protruded spots on the body (parasites)

- stringy extension from the vent (intestinal worms)

- cottony puffs or white/gray color patches on the body (fungus)

- lesions or damage on body or near edge of tail (actual or potential bacterial infection)

- overly thin body (internal parasites or fish tuberculosis)

Livebearers with strange growths should not be purchased. Look instead for healthy, active fish.

- shimmying in one place rather than swimming, often with clamped fins (acclimation problem or ammonia poisoning)

Indeed, passing on the whole tank, and any other tanks that are on the same central filtration system, is not a bad idea if it is a parasitic or fungal issue, or if many fish are dead or dying.

What to Look For

A good, trustworthy pet shop—one that uses reliable wholesalers, acclimates and treats its fish well, provides sound advice, and has patience with customers—is an enormous asset for the hobbyist. Stores like these are well worth the extra price you may pay for their fish. Healthy fish are always good value.

Ask the pet store operator how long your chosen fish have been in their tanks. I like to wait a few days at least before purchasing new arrivals to make sure they acclimate properly. Of course, a unique fancy swordtail or fabulous new guppy may sell out quickly, so sometimes it is worth the risk to make the purchase. If the fish do not make it, I tend not to blame the store here in these situations and not look for a refund because of my gamble.

I also look for fish that are active. Even with shy or reclusive livebearer species, the approach of the net should elicit an escape or curiosity reaction if the fish is healthy.

Other Sources for Livebearers

Hard-to-find livebearers require looking at sources apart from your local pet store. Wild-type and higher-quality fancy livebearers are generally found through aquarium societies (fish clubs), livebearer organization trading posts, and private breeders who advertise in magazines and on the Internet via their own hatcheries or auction sites. Local aquarium societies should be your first choice. You will be able to pick out and bring home newly bagged fish that are probably already accustomed to your local tap water, and that have been cared for by a seasoned aquarist. If you buy from a source outside your area, you will have to deal with the added stress (and cost) of shipped fish. Whatever fish you acquire, I recommend trying to obtain more females than males. Male livebearers will endlessly pursue females to mate, so having more than one female around gives each female a break from the chase now and then.

Getting Them Home

If you make your selection via a pet store, make sure the attendant bags your fish in a large bag with one-third

Ignore any advice you may get to float your bagged fish in your aquarium. This does NOT properly acclimate the fish to your tank's water.

water and two-thirds air. The large amount of air space facilitates oxygen and carbon dioxide gas exchange. I also pass on the large dollop of sticky water conditioner that some stores squirt liberally into the bag before tying it. However, if they are using an ammonia neutralizer, that can be beneficial. But request only a drop or two. Overdosing chemicals can further stress your new animal.

Whether they come from retail outlet or fish club, get your fish home as soon as possible! Avoid direct sunlight and heat, and keep them away from chills during the trip. During winter months, bring along a portable insulated or rigid foam board cooler to maintain temperature and to keep them dark (which keeps them calmer and thus creates less waste in their bag).

Acclimation

Regardless of how or where you acquired your new livebearers, you will need to start acclimating them to your aquarium water before adding them to your tank. There are two ways to accomplish this.

The most common way is immediate placement. Place the fish bag at the bottom of your dedicated aquarium bucket and gently release the fish and water. Add one cup of aquarium water to the bucket using a well-rinsed clean cup (I keep one dedicated only to aquarium use, or I use a new foam or paper cup). Add a drop of your ammonia-neutralizing water conditioner. Add a little more water *only* if the fish is not completely covered.

Wait ten minutes and add another cup of your aquarium water. Now repeat this process every five minutes.

After 30 minutes total time in the bucket your fish can be netted. With your hand over the net opening, place the entire net with fish into your aquarium and let them find their own way out. Never shake or push a fish out of a net and plop them in the water. And never add the bucket water to the aquarium; dispose of it either down a drain or outside your home.

Note we are not advocating the popular "float the bag and release" method advocated by some pet stores and aquarium books. This will only acclimate the fish to your water's temperature, not its chemical makeup. This may also release potentially pathogen-seeded water into your aquarium.

The other method of acclimation, if space permits, and the best way to avoid introducing a disease to your established aquarium, is to place your new arrival into a small spare aquarium that will serve the dual-function of a quarantine and hospital tank. For livebearers, a 2.5-gallon (10-liter) aquarium works fine for single specimens or small pairs, while a 5- or 10-gallon (20- or 40-liter) works for trios and up. This aquarium should have all the established filtration mentioned in the previous chapters. Usually this can be accomplished by borrowing some plants from the main tank and using half the biological media from the established aquarium. You will need a small, gentle filter, heater, and light as well. Acclimate the fish in the aforementioned way and observe for at least one week for any sign of disease before adding them to their permanent home.

Playing Doctor

Even the most dedicated and careful hobbyist encounters a sick fish every now and then. It is amazing how rare this event can be among seasoned hobbyists, but it does occur. Usually a diseased or sick fish in a healthy aquarium is actually an animal at

Sick fish should be removed from your main aquarium and placed in a separate quarantine tank.

the end of its natural life, and its immunity and defense systems have ceased working properly. The popular livebearing fish rarely live more than three years, and five years is the upper range. Lower temperatures will extend their lives by slowing their metabolism.

Livebearers are very hardy, but they do suffer from certain ailments more than others. A new fish and their pet store water can harbor pathogens not observed during the selection process. A sudden temperature change or virulent pathogen can sometimes invade even the healthiest of aquariums. A fish that is a runt or victim of aggression from another fish will have lower resistance to disease.

Here now we will discuss the most common livebearer ailments you might encounter.

Ich or White Spot Disease
The ich parasite, so called because of the scientific name of the causative organism, is a commonly encountered protozoan parasite that has a substrate-dwelling, a free-swimming, and an actively parasitic stage. Healthy fish resist infection, but sudden chilling can lower resistance, so ich (pronounced "ick") is commonly encountered during the change of seasons. Ich appears as tiny white spots all over the fish's body, including the fins.

For treatment, raise the temperature to 84°F (29°C) degrees to expedite the parasite's life cycle, and use an ich medication as per label directions. After cure, bring your temperature back down slowly over several days. I

SMALL FRY

Keeping Your Fish Healthy Is Easy!
Once your aquarium is set up correctly and working well, keeping your fish healthy is as easy as 1-2-3:
1. Feed just a little every day and make sure everyone eats.
2. Change some of the water every week with an older person to help you.
3. Don't make your aquarium crowded or keep bullying fish.

prefer to treat the entire aquarium for an ich infection.

Intestinal Worms
Intestinal worms are very common in wild fish that have been starved prior to shipment, especially with wild-type livebearers. Symptoms vary but can include a thinning body and lethargy, unexplained multiple deaths, and a thread-like protrusion (the worm itself) from the vent. There are medications available to treat intestinal worms. I prefer to treat the entire tank and repeat the treatment three weeks later.

Bacterial Infections
These rare but highly contagious infections usually appear as a graying swatch over the back of a livebearer.

The Salt Myth

Hobbyists are often given the poor advice to add some salt to livebearer tanks, especially for mollies. This only creates a less hardy fish in the long run and a difficult-to-dose aquarium that cannot support vegetative filtration as salt concentrations build up over time.

Most of our aquarium livebearers hail from areas rich in limestone (calcium carbonate). If your tap water is not calcium- or magnesium-hard, you can create these natural conditions by using crushed coral or limestone rocks in your aquarium. Most livebearers benefit from this approach, and your vegetative filtration will not be negatively affected.

All infected fish should be removed immediately and treated with antibiotics in the hospital tank. Make sure to follow the package directions to the letter and do not end treatment early. The host tank and other fish can then be sanitized gently with an appropriate disinfectant.

Tail Rot

Tail rot is common in fancy guppies housed with nippy tankmates. Observe your tank from a distance to determine whether nippiness is the cause (some loaches are notorious for this behavior when their surroundings are quiet and not being observed). This can also be a warning sign of poor water quality or a buildup of harmful bacteria in the substrate. One of the tea tree extracts sold in pet shops, along with more frequent water changes, has proved expeditious in the healing process. A hospital tank for the injured fish (or a quarantine tank for the bully fish) comes in very handy here.

Shimmying and Clamped Fins

Most common in highly inbred and thus more delicate mollies. This strange behavior is attributed to three factors:

- osmotic shock resulting from a quick transition from salted fish farm or shipping water to municipal pet shop water
- ammonia sensitivity
- crowded and sub-optimal conditions

Best approach here is to avoid buying fish like this in the first place. If shimmying and clamping does occur, slowly raise the temperature, perform a water change, check your ammonia and nitrite levels, and make sure there is enough calcium carbonate in your water via your tap or through the use of limestone rocks or crushed coral. And remember: sailfin mollies in particular need their space! Don't crowd them in anything less than a 24-inch (60-cm) long tank to a pair.

Chapter 6

Livebearer Aquariums

One of the best aspects of the livebearer hobby is the many ways to specialize. No other field of interest in the aquarium or pond hobbies offers more ways to enjoy your pastime, or provides a fit for your particular personality type, like the livebearer hobby.

Catfish of the genus Corydoras *make excellent tankmates in a community aquarium.*

For example, the artisan may enjoy bringing a slice of nature into their home with a beautifully planted Zen-style tank. Most livebearers are perfect for planted tanks, as they pick at algae, don't destroy plants, and provide small but solid waste for fertilization. In contrast, the scientist type may set up a series of stark breeding tanks to explore genetics or attempt to create a new variety of fish.

Livebearers may also serve the entrepreneur in us. You may find a market in your local shop or online for certain livebearers, and set up a mini hatchery in your home. The competitor needs the most efficient system of all, complete with strict culling, feeding, and water changing regimens, as they develop their fish for the show circuit and its awards.

Lastly we have the collector, which is the one attribute shared by all serious fish people. They are characterized by having multiple tanks, often evolving to a separate fish room. This is especially evident among those who join aquarium societies.

There are many ways to enjoy the livebearer hobby. Let's review your options.

The Community Aquarium

This is the most common type of tank setup and the one we all start with. Initially it is a hodgepodge or fish, plants, ornaments, and colored gravel, often with disastrous results when the fish's compatibility and requirements are not considered before setup time.

Most livebearers make perfect community residents. The majority are hardy and peaceful. The fancy forms we see in shops and shows are some of the most colorful and elaborate of freshwater fish; these factors, combined with their fecundity, help maintain the interest of the hobbyist.

If you plan to keep different livebearer species or color forms from the same genus, be aware that there is a strong possibility that they will interbreed. If you plan to keep wild-type species in a community tank, *include only one species per genus.*

The best fish suitable for community tanks with livebearers are the diminutive bottom-feeding *Corydoras* catfish and the gentle algae-eating *Otocinclus* catfish. Both *must* be fed a specialized food, however, to supplement their diet and maintain good health.

Many books recommend some of the popular barb or tetra species for livebearer community tanks, but these active fish can be nippy on the livebearers with elaborate finnage. Also, they will eat some or all of your livebearer fry (which may be a good thing when you take into account how often livebearers reproduce!). Some barbs are good algae eaters, though.

There are other fish, however, that are small-mouthed and relatively gentle as livebearer neighbors. The white cloud is a small schooling fish that often flock-breeds right in the community tank without eating its own fry. The harlequin rasbora is another striking fish and makes a great display in an aquarium.

When stocking a community tank, it is important to keep fish of relatively the same size. Otherwise, you are essentially creating an underwater buffet for the larger specimens. Livebearer fry are particularly tempting in this regard. If you do want larger fish, a pair of small cichlids, from the docile and hardy keyhole cichlid and the even smaller curviceps, can be included in livebearer communities. In a heavily planted aquarium, some livebearer fry will survive—especially if they are top-dwelling species like most of the poeciliids. Indeed, this supplemental diet of stray livebearer fry can help condition a pair of egglaying fish for spawning.

Do *not* keep angelfish in livebearer tanks. On more than one occasion I have witnessed an adult angelfish literally inhale full-grown female guppies!

A Livebearer Community

How about a community aquarium for just livebearers? These work best when you select species that inhabit different zones of the aquarium, such as top-dwelling knife livebearers, *Alfaro* spp., with

The keyhole cichlid.

bottom-dwelling humpbacked limias, *Limia nigrofasciata*, or rainbow goodeids, *Characodon* spp., and mid-water *Xiphophorus*. The key here is to choose species whose members are aggressive only towards each other, not to fish of other species. Also important is not to mix species in the same genus. This results in hybrid fish that are generally undesirable and contaminate an otherwise pure species or line. *One species per genus in any aquarium, please!*

Species Tanks

The livebearer specialist invariably moves on to single-species tanks. This removes the stress that other species can create and ensures that more fry survive. Sometimes these aquariums are aquascaped based on the species' natural habitat.

This type of setup is particularly important for species maintenance for extinct-in-nature or endangered fishes. This is just one way hobbyists can do their part to keep a species alive for possible re-introduction or just conservation. All you need is a simple small aquarium to do this for most of the endangered or extinct-in-nature livebearers. Keeping just one aquarium for an endangered species is one of the most meaningful and important things a hobbyist can do with the aquarium pastime.

A popular species aquarium is the multi-generational colony tank. In this aquarium the entire cycle of life is completed—from mating to birth to maturity to death—all in the

SMALL FRY

A Livebearer Among Dinosaurs

Who says science isn't interesting? Dinosaur fans know that these "terrible lizards" became extinct at the end of the Cretaceous period, about 65 million years ago. Another group of animals thought to have gone extinct at this time was a highly evolved order of fish called coelacanths. These fish were related to lungfish and tetrapods. They were very successful fish for over 300 million years, with many genera and species, before the fossil record indicated they were no more.

Then in 1938 a coelacanth was discovered in the catch of a South African fishing vessel. Further catches of live specimens, along with underwater photography, proved that this living fossil, referred to as *Latimeria chalumnae*, survived extinction deep in the ocean's depths. It reaches over 6 feet (2 m) in length and weighs a whopping 175 pounds (79 kg)!

Now the oldest living lineage of jawed fish on the planet, the coelacanth was also discovered to be a livebearer, delivering broods of 5 to 25 fry after 13 months of gestation. It is *not* suitable for the aquarium, however!

same tank. I particularly enjoy this approach, as it is this system that allows you, the hobbyist, to travel along with your fish and watch them grow and develop. In many ways it is not unlike your first aquarium. Some of the most knowledgeable hobbyists I know are the new ones with that first tank. They take the time—and with great pleasure—to observe their animals. A colony tank is very much an observation aquarium where you really get to know a species. It brings us back to basics and the wonders (and joy) of that first fish tank.

Livebearer colony tanks will differ according to the species you maintain. Some will be highlighted by aggression, such as a tankful of *Belonesox belizanus*, who will eat each other if not fed enough live food! Others will be a near model of peaceful co-existence, such as with *Xiphophorus maculatus*. Many will

develop a hierarchical pecking order, as the alpha male slowly emerges to dominate the colony as seen in some limia, swordtail, and variatus colonies. But even here, a small runty male, via a sneak mating here and there, will find a way to pass on his genes. Fascinating stuff here that really makes you re-consider the complexities of livebearers versus their reputation as bread and butter fish.

Successful colony tanks require long aquariums. Twenty-gallon (80-liter) "longs" (30 inches, 75 cm) will suit most of the popular Central and South American species, although small, non-aggressive livebearer species can do well in 10- or 15-gallon (40- or 60-liter) tanks. A colony of the tiny native American *Heterandria formosa* can be accomplished in an unheated 2.5-gallon (10-liter) aquarium 12 inches long (30 cm), and thus is perfect for desktop setups. But longer aquariums better

This planted 20-gallon (80-liter) long tank is perfect to display beautiful Xiphophorus *swordtails.*

Heterandria formosa, *a small livebearer that will do well in desktop aquaria.*

allow for territories for mating, birth, escape, and socialization.

The decor for a livebearer colony tank should include a combination of floating and bottom plants. This is for both water quality and practical reasons. The exact mix will depend on your species. Newborn *Poecilia* fry usually head for the surface, while *Xiphophorus* and stream-dwelling livebearers stay near the bottom. Clusters of small stones around the tank are helpful here as well. Java fern or willow mosses (*Fontinalis* spp.) make for a good grazing/hiding place for fry. A few sprigs placed throughout the tank and covered with a light coating of gravel create a nice carpet after a few weeks. More fry survive under these conditions.

Plant or rock clusters in the back corners and sides of the aquarium make for handy nurseries for females and fry to congregate. I emphasize that you consider the use of small perforated pots sold for ponds or even small clay pots if you plan on harvesting or thinning out your colony. Netting out livebearers from a permanently planted aquarium is usually quite disruptive and always vexing!

This leaves the center of the colony tank as an open area for courtship, mating, sparring, and other social behavior. It is not uncommon for your first drop of fry to be eaten by the larger fish in the tank. But with plenty of cover, combined with regular good feedings (at least twice a day), some of the fry will survive. The other fish in the tank will eventually grow accustomed to sharing their space with young fish, and the colony will go into production. Sometimes it's a good idea to raise the first drop of fry separately for the colony to gain some size, ensuring a good brood of little fish for the adults to get used to.

Another protection method employed by some livebearer breeders is to utilize the plastic tank dividers commonly sold in pet shops. But instead of using the pin-holed plastic sheet that comes with the divider, the hobbyist purchases an inexpensive hard plastic mesh sheet, cut to size, from a store that sells knitting supplies. The larger holes in these sheets enable fry to escape from hungry adults. This may be especially helpful for carnivorous livebearers from the poeciliid tribe Gambusini (*Brachyrhaphis, Gambusia,* and *Belonesox* species).

If you research your fish carefully before setting up your colony tank, you may be able to re-create their biotope, at least in terms of color and basic topography. Then you may better understand why a particular livebearer is shaped or colored the way it is. For example, put some swordtails in a river-style overflow tank and watch them leap effortlessly over the waterfall. Or watch a *Belonesox* ambush its prey from behind a plant.

The Breeder Setup

The creation of a new fancy strain of livebearer, one that no one else has developed, is the dream of many hobbyists. Some livebearians enjoy the thrill of competition by breeding and raising champion show fish. Both pursuits require a more specialized livebearer aquarium system.

Livebearers produce a lot of fry. If you decide to keep them, you must prepare for the copious offspring beforehand.

Breeding Techniques

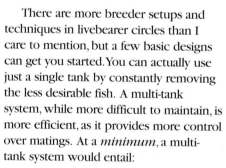

There are basically three types of breeding techniques to assist you in developing or maintaining the fancy livebearer you desire. Inbreeding is when you cross two closely related fish, such brother-sister, father-daughter, etc. This is used to fix a trait such as color or fin shape. At its simplest, inbreeding entails selecting the best female and male in your stock for the empty breeding tank.

Line-breeding is a form of inbreeding in which the fry are separated into two or more batches, eventually creating duplicate four-tank breeder setups. This is desirable when you have an expensive or rare fish that you want to ensure does not weaken over time through excessive inbreeding. Every few generations you cross the two lines to create hybrid vigor but maintain the qualities you desire. Out-crossing is what happens in a mixed guppy community tank. Two different strains with different color or finnage are crossed. Often the progeny of such unrelated fish are large, robust animals (hybrid vigor again). This is where new strains develop, but then the hard work begins of trying to fix the strain through inbreeding.

There are more breeder setups and techniques in livebearer circles than I care to mention, but a few basic designs can get you started. You can actually use just a single tank by constantly removing the less desirable fish. A multi-tank system, while more difficult to maintain, is more efficient, as it provides more control over matings. At a *minimum*, a multi-tank system would entail:

- Tank for your mature breeders, preferably with the sexes separated. Keep temperatures on the low end of the spectrum to maintain longevity, and feed a diet lower in protein (try goldfish diets).
- Tank for breeding, birthing, and raising fry. Maintain higher temperatures to accelerate birth and growth.
- Female grow-out tank.
- Male grow-out tank.

Optimally feed the fry and juveniles multiple times per day with a higher-protein diet, including micro dry food, freeze-dried or live daphnia, and live newly hatched brine shrimp. (The latter is the staple food of show folk.)

Note that I did not recommend the use of breeding traps. These contraptions are usually too small and stressful for females. If you are in a pinch for space, the net-type breeding traps offer the best water circulation and temporary space for an expectant mother or to protect a batch of fry. Alternatively, a 1-gallon (4-liter) or larger fish bowl with lots of live plants like anacharis makes a good birthing environment.

The Fishroom

The next level in the aquarium hobby, after multiple tanks start appearing throughout the house, is to move your hobby downstairs to a basement or bottom-level room. Here one's aquatic collection can be housed together and enjoyed. Heating becomes efficient in an enclosed space, and water changes can generally be done more quickly and with access to a nearby sink or drain. Many serious hobbyists see their fishrooms as an escape to a little slice of the tropics. I particularly enjoyed my fishroom in the dead of winter for these reasons.

But fishrooms can have their drawbacks. They can allow the accumulation of fish and tanks that exceed the time available by the hobbyist unless other parts of life are forsaken or cut back. Many fishrooms turn a hobby into a laborious task, with not enough time to just sit and enjoy your fish. Fishrooms can be isolating too. They can keep you apart from your family right in your own home. Spreading your aquariums across your home, although less efficient, prevents this problem. So does incorporating your fishroom as part of a larger family space.

If you still desire a fishroom, and can manage your time and collection wisely, there are many blueprints on how to do it. For homeowners, the obvious spot is one's basement or a bottom-level room. The concrete slabs found here support a lot of weight, and nearby slop sinks or floor drains can make messy water changes less stressful.

But you need not find a room or a spot in your basement to enjoy a dedicated space for your fish. Livebearers, most being smaller and

Fishrooms allow you to keep many tanks of the fish you love.

Livebearer Species at Risk

Abbreviations
At Risk in Nature (AR), Conservation Dependent (CD), Conservation Priority (CP), Critically Endangered (CR), Data Deficient (DD), Endangered (EN), Extinct (EX), Extinct in the Wild (EW), Least Concern (LC), Near Threatened (NT), Not Evaluated (NE), Vulnerable (VU)

Species	Common Name	Classification
Allodontichthys hubbsi	Whitepatched splitfin	EN
Allodontichthys polylepis*		EW
Allodontichthys tamazulae	Peppered splitfin, Tuxpan splitfin	VU
Allodontichthys zonistius*		VU
Alloophorus robustus	Bulldog goodeid	VU
Allotoca catarinae*		VU
Allotoca diazi*		EN
Allotoca dugesii	Bumblebee allotoca, opal allotoca	EN
Allotoca goslinei	Banded allotoca	EN
Allotoca maculata	Opal goodeid	CR/EW/CP
Allotoca meeki*		EW
Allotoca zacapuensis*		EW
Ameca splendens	Butterfly goodeid	EW/CR
Ataeniobius toweri	Bluetail goodeid	EN/EW

Species	Common Name	Classification
Chapalichthys pardalis	Polkadot goodeid, polkadot splitfin, leopard goodeid	CR/AR
Chapalichthys peraticus*		EW
Characodon audax	Black prince, bold characodon	VU/EW
Characodon lateralis	Rainbow goodeid	EN/EW
Girardinichthys multiradiatus	Darkedged splitfin	VU/EN
Girardinichthys viviparus	Black sailfin goodeid, Mexclapique	CR/EW/CP
Goodea gracilis	Dusky splitfin	VU
Hubbsina turneri	Highland splitfin	CR/EW/CP
Ilyodon cortesae*		VU
Ilyodon whitei	Balsas splitfin, White's ilyodon	CR/VU
Neophoorus (Allotoca) regalis*		EW
Nomorhamphus weberi*		VU
Phallichthys quadripunctatus*		CP
Poecilia latipunctata	Rio Tamesí molly, broadspotted molly	CR
Poecilia sulphuraria	Sulphur molly	CR
Skiffia bilineata	Twoline skiffia	EW
Skiffia francesae	Golden skiffia, tiro	EW / AR
Skiffia lermae*		EN

Livebearer Species at Risk (continued)

Species	Common Name	Classification
Skiffia multipunctata	Speckled sawfin goodeid, spotted skiffia	EN
Xenoophorus captivus	Relict splitfin, green goodeid, solo goodeid, yellow goodeid	EN/EW
*Xenotaenia resolanae**		VU
Xenotoca eiseni	Redtail goodeid	EN
Xenotoca melanosoma	Black splitfin, dusky goodeid, blue-bellied goodeid	VU
Xiphophorus couchianus	Monterrey platyfish	EW/CD
Xiphophorus gordoni	Northern platyfish	EN
Xiphophorus meyeri	Musquiz platyfish	EW/CD
Zoogoneticus quitzeoensis	Picotee goodeid	VU
Zoogoneticus tequila	Tequila goodeid	EW

Information taken from www.carespreservation.com
*species does not have a common name

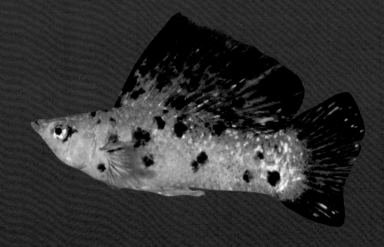

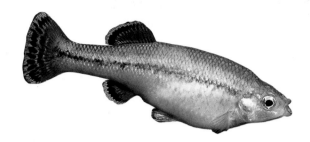

less aggressive than, say, most cichlids and catfish, are perfect for a variety of spaces. Consider these alternatives to a fish room:

- that spare closet
- a shed or covered rack system (for hobbyists in the deep south, sub-tropical, and tropical areas)
- along a strong bookcase with center vertical supports
- a corner rack of stained wood in any room
- the garage

The core of any room or space for fish is a custom-built rack system. Some fishrooms are just a collection of aquariums on stands, with perhaps heavy-duty bracketed shelving mounted to the studs in a wall for supplies, books, and aquariums of 10 gallons (40 liters) or less. But multi-level rack systems are more common and allow more aquariums in the same space. Getting involved with a local aquarium society, and visiting several members' fishrooms, will expose the various techniques.

Fish racks can be built using metal or 2 x 4 lumber. I like strong, thick lag screws when working with wood. Even stronger are dove-tail joints so wood rests on wood. An easier but less pretty option is stacked cinderblocks threaded with lumber. These can be easily re-arranged at a later date. Most aquariums from 15 to 45 gallons (30 to 90 liters) are 12.5 inches (32 cm) deep and this makes a good front-to-back depth for your rack planning. Vertical

center braces are not a bad idea either.

Each tier or shelf is then topped off with a half inch (1 cm) or more thick sheet of plywood, preferably sealed with two coats of polyurethane. This sheet of wood will help insulate the bottom of the tank too. You may have to use wood shims under the rack's legs to level the system.

Lastly, screw your rack to the wall's wood studs for extra stability. If you live in an apartment or condominium, it behooves you to place the aquariums against an outside supporting wall, preferably utilizing the corners. Remember: just the water alone weighs about 8 pounds per gallon.

I prefer two tiered racks—one slightly above and one slightly below eye level—but most hobbyists employ three or four tiers (I always find the inconvenient bottom and top tanks are mostly ignored). Often these are placed in "steps" with tanks slightly overlapping each other to maximize the vertical space.

Tier systems are also helpful for varying temperature: cool water livebearers like goodeids for the lower racks; South American and Asian species for the upper warmer region; Centrals in the middle. Livebearer fishrooms, with their more frequent

The author's son investigating a pair of plastic utility-tub fish ponds. Fish tubs are a simple and enjoyable outdoor addition to your collection.

fry production, benefit from an upper tier of grow-out tanks, whose higher temperatures encourage faster growth. The copious amount of fry also means that a livebearer fishroom needs to have a good supply of baby brine shrimp and/or daphnia available (live, frozen, or freeze-dried, in that order of preference).

Livebearers do well in small, shallow tanks, which allow more tiers and rows on the rack, as well as easier viewing. The most versatile aquarium for the fishroom or rack, in my opinion, is the ubiquitous 20-gallon (80-liter) long (30 inches, 76 cm) which is low enough to create multiple tiers and rows of tanks that are serviceable, but long enough to afford breeding and raising up variety of species (including many cichlids), as well as create multi-generational colonies. The 15-gallon (30-liter) tanks,

at 24 inches (60 cm), are good too for most livebearer racks as they can be paired next to each other to span the width of a standard fluorescent shop light (48 inches, 121 cm).

Either way, please measure your available space by subtracting the space your rack will take up, and then decide on which tanks fit your footprint. Remember that you will have more length to work with on the top of the rack than you will in lower tiers because they will be between your rack supports and center braces. Plan accordingly!

Lighting for fishrooms is usually done with cheap and efficient fluorescent shop lighting. Try to find one with an electronic ballast for lower running cost and longer bulb life. Heating can be centralized to save additional costs, although a well-insulated room is advised if one goes this route.

Filtration for fishrooms usually consists of a central air pump of linear or piston design, hooked up to a series of box or sponge filters via PVC pipe and tubing. Smaller setups do just fine with a standard vibrating diaphragm pump. I prefer one with a rheostat, so I can adjust the electricity flow and air output without straining the pump. The new internal power filters currently on the market provide a heat source, and this may be a good option if you do not centralize your heating.

Water changes are always the fishkeeper's lament. The use of small water pumps with garden hose hookups, as well as automatic water changing devices that attach to your faucet, are options to make this necessary task less laborious. A trend now in the United States is to build central water-changing systems utilizing PVC piping that attaches to your faucet or water line (gravity or pump siphon) to drain and fill your entire fishroom at once.

As you see, fishrooms and fish racks are a hobby in and of themselves!

Fish Tubs and Water Gardens

An age-old aspect of fishkeeping has been enjoying a renaissance of sorts in the first decade of the new millennium: outdoor summer fish tubs! This was a common practice during the Golden Age of the hobby in the first half of the twentieth century, and many old-timers still utilize nature's bounty to accelerate growth, mating, and the colors of their fish. It also let's you enjoy a pond with just a little space, no digging, and even less maintenance than an aquarium.

Most of all, it's just plain fun, and it allows you to enjoy the outside without abandoning your fish inside. Livebearers are particularly well suited to outdoor breeding and maintenance. Most withstand a broader temperature range and are hardier than other tropical freshwater fish.

A summer fish tub for livebearers is at its simplest with a free-standing round plastic container of at least 20 gallons (80 liters). Other shapes will bow and tear on the sides. Black weather-proof plastic barrel liners sold in pond and hardware stores provide both the necessary depth for temperature control and the bottom space for multiple planting pots. Also common are 34-gallon (136-liter) round shallow pools with planting shelves. Both are free-standing. Least expensive and completely serviceable are the high round utility tubs sold in discount stores for a few dollars. Different colors are available throughout the year, so you can find one that complements your outside living space or garden.

Vegetative filtration will be the engine of your summer fish tub, with the sun and fish waste providing the fuel. The list of

Keep a watchful eye when children are around container fish ponds.

recommended plants is led by the floating water hyacinth. This quickly reproducing plant provides shade from the sun, protection from chilling winds, grazing and fry protection areas from its long, thick roots, beautiful flowers, and highly efficient filtration. (Depending on where you live, however, the water hyacinth might be illegal to keep, as in the wild the plant can reproduce so quickly that it impedes navigation.) Other good plants include floating water lettuce, native American cattails and pickerels, which unlike other pond plants thrive in deep waters. For aesthetics, you can include a hardy *Nymphaea* water lily. (My recommendation would be the profuse-blooming helova for small tubs, or sulphuria for large tubs.)

What makes these plants so much more effective filters than regular aquarium plants is that they grow emersed; their foliage resides above the water, where carbon dioxide and natural light are plentiful for maximum photosynthesis and metabolism of water wastes. The plants mentioned here are particularly good at metabolizing wastes.

In your summer livebearer tub, food will also be in abundance. Insects and their larvae, introduced daphnia, and algae will provide very natural food sources. Feeding with prepared fish foods daily is helpful, but there are no worries if you skip a meal or even go on vacation. At the end of the season, you will be amazed how fast those fry you placed in that tub in June grew by tear-down time in September, and how

Summer Fish Tub Pests

Mosquito larvae: no problem at all if you are keeping larvae-eating fish like livebearers. Indeed, your pond could become a mosquito control station, as egg rafts laid here have almost no chance of eventually generating flying mosquitoes. I like to use one of the bacterial anti-mosquito briquettes in my water gardens as an added measure.

Dragonfly larvae: not a problem if the fish tub is broken down at the end of the season. A few fry may be eaten, but young dragonfly larvae prefer mosquito larvae as the main meal.

Raccoons: can wreak havoc in a pond by removing the plants and making a mess, not to mention eating the fish that are big enough to attract their attention. Best to use a humane trap sold at hardware stores. You can also place a few pieces of wood or wire mesh on your summer tub at night and use bricks to weigh them down so raccoons can't get in.

colorful adult fish are compared to their tank-raised cousins.

Some planning and a few precautions are required before you proceed with a livebearer water garden. Give a good washing with baking soda and salt to your new tubs to remove any residues. Rinse well before filling. Positioning the tub will take some trial and error over a few seasons to find your yard's (or balcony or window's) "sweet spot." You want full sun or diffused sun. Western states may require some shading for their tubs. A tub on concrete or asphalt will hold in heat better at night and as the season gets cooler, but it will also not cool down as quickly on hot days as one placed on earthen ground.

When you acquire plants, soak them for 24 hours in a fluke tablet solution to destroy any hydra and other parasites (which are rare but can be deadly). After rinsing, place them in perforated planting baskets with aquarium gravel. You want their roots to grow out of the baskets to filter the water.

Timing when to put out your fish and take them back inside is important. You can start your tub in the spring, as the plants will start growing. You may need some tablet fertilizer at this stage since there are no fish or food wastes to be utilized. I like to put out my livebearers when the day temperature reaches 70°F (21°C) or higher consistently for several days. Over the summer your fish will adjust well to the slowly changing temperatures and you can take them in before the first frost date in your area. Goodeids can stay out longer. Refer to specifications given for individual species in Chapter 7. As an example, here in the northern New Jersey area my season generally runs three months, from the second half of June to July 4th through September 15th to October 1st. Watch your forecast and don't tempt fate!

Children can help with the maintenance of your fish pond with guidance and supervision.

Who Am I?

The phenomenon of bearing live young occurs across 56 families of fish—14 of which are "bony fish," the ones we keep in aquariums (unless we happen to keep sharks or rays). But only four of those 14 families are of particular importance to aquarium hobbyists: the poeciliids, the goodeids, the anablepids, and the halfbeaks. Each one is unique and offers many species to observe, breed, and enjoy. This chapter will provide details on many of these wonderful species.

To learn the care requirements for this Brachyrhaphis roseni *(male pictured), see page 74.*

For each species we will provide the following information and recommendations:

- **Scientific Name:** genus + species
- **Common Name(s):** name(s) by which a fish is known in commercial or hobby circles
- **Native Geography:** place/country of origin
- **Biotope:** habitat description. Trying to match your aquarium to your species's natural environment usually leads to better breeding success and more appropriate behavior. For example, livebearers from calm or still waters would probably appreciate a power filter with a diffuse and non-turbulent outflow, or a gently bubbling sponge or box filter, while species from rapidly moving waters appreciate a filter with a directed powerful output—or perhaps a powerhead or two to provide current. Some livebearers have evolved in more heavily planted waters, so lots of plastic or live plants are helpful for them in an aquarium.

- **Size:** approximate adult male and female sizes, and notable differences
- **Minimum Tank Size:** to house an adult trio (two females, one male). If the aquarium is at least 10 gallons (and 20 inches) in capacity (40 liters and 50 cm), and unless noted otherwise in the species description, other residents can include small *Corydoras* or *Otocinclus* catfish. A trio of small tetras, rasboras, danios, or minnows can be included, but keep in mind that this will lower the number of surviving newborn fry in your

tank (not always a bad thing in a productive livebearer aquarium!). Remember: larger is always better when it comes to tank size.

- **Diet:** listed in order of importance for a balanced diet

- **Temperature:** acceptable ranges for long-term maintenance. A 5-degree change above and below these ranges is usually well tolerated if it (1) happens gradually, and (2) is only temporary, such as the case with night versus day temperatures in summer water gardens or greenhouses. Sudden or prolonged temperature changes outside the recommended range should be avoided.

Family Poeciliidae

The poeciliids are one of the most successful and evolved families of freshwater fish on the planet, and the ones you will encounter at every pet shop. Years of selective breeding have made them colorful staples of the hobby and show circuit.

Poeciliids often demonstrate a high tolerance for brackish and, in many species, even marine conditions. Livebearing poeciliids evolved from egg-laying toothcarps in South America. This is evidenced in their close taxonomical relationship to the Amazonian Fluviphylax as well as African lampeyes and pantanodons. Multiple radiations to northern landmasses may

have begun about 44 million years ago.

Livebearing poeciliids are native to the Western Hemisphere only. But they have a broad distribution, with close to 200 species ranging from the Mid-Atlantic United States down to Argentina. They can now be found in waters all over the world—from Saudi Arabia to California's Salton Sea—as ornamental, accidental, or intentional introductions to fight mosquitoes. This is usually to the detriment of native species and their ecosystems.

The success of the poeciliids results from several key biological features. Foremost is their efficient reproductive system. Males possess a modified flexible anal fin known as a gonopodium, an elaborate structure with a series of bony hooks, clasps, and/or flaps for securing to the female's vent (gonopodium anatomy is a key criterion for differentiating poeciliid species). This allows their

sperm to be delivered directly into the female's egg cavity as packets—often without the female's participation—

rather than sprayed haphazardly over eggs laid in open water as with most other fish.

Equally remarkable is the female poeciliid's uncanny ability to store sperm packets to fertilize broods for many months thereafter. The females then either deliver large broods of fry about every 30 days, or smaller broods over several days in an assembly-line process known as superfetation (higher temperatures reduce these times, while lower temps increase the duration). Many amateur hobbyists are bewildered the first time they discover baby fish in an aquarium where only a single fish has resided for quite a while!

The small size of most poeciliids has also been an evolutionary plus, as it enables them to inhabit shallow and isolated water bodies and colonize them with just a single pregnant female. Most poecillids possess a versatile mouth for feeding as well. Fleshy and bony sections allow them to capitalize on a variety of surfaces where food can be found. The upturned mouth of most species makes them capable surface skimmers where insects lay their egg rafts. All these biological features have led to the poeciliids' surprisingly fast adaptation to changing environments, predators, and food sources, as well as the evolution of many new species.

Okay, let's review the most common genera in the family Poeciliidae and some popular species contained in those genera.

Alfaro

A genus comprising two species commonly referred to as the knife-edge livebearers due to their jagged posterior scales. Gonopodium structure suggests it's a primordial poeciliid, but recent molecular DNA analysis implies it is more recently evolved. Reproduction is via ovoviviparity, with elongated fry that are slow to mature but are rarely pursued by their parents.

Livebearer Reproduction Refresher

True Vivipary: mother provides continuous nourishment and gas exchange to the developing fetus.

Ovovivipary: nourishment for the embryo is provided via a yolk sac in the fertilized egg, with some gas exchange via the mother's womb.

Superfetation: the fertilization of eggs and subsequent birth occur over several days instead of all at once, resulting in an assembly-line process of maturation and birth.

Alfaro cultratus

Alfaro cultratus

Common Name: knife livebearer
Native Geography: Atlantic drainage
from southern Guatemala
through Panama
Biotope: flowing rainforest streams,
often swift
Size: males 2.3 inches (6 cm); females 3
inches (8 cm)
Minimum Tank Size: 30 inches
(90 cm) long
Diet: insectivore; carnivore; flakes
Temperature: 76° to 83°F (24° to 28°C)
　　Unfairly labeled primitive, *A. cultratus* displays a keen memory
and interesting courtship behavior.
It supposedly rubs its elongated
ventral fins on the head of the female
to communicate its intentions. It is
aggressive toward its own species, and
is easily frightened. With an elongated
and compressed body, and greenish
hue, it makes a unique lively resident
for the upper portion of the livebearer
aquarium. Introduced to the aquarium
hobby by James K. Langhammer of
Detroit. Its sister species, the orangey *A. huberi*, is more stocky and delicate, but
enjoys similar water conditions.

Belonesox

A genus of one or maybe two species
of ambush predators from Central
America. With its sharp teeth, large
body, and craving for flesh, *Belonesox*
bust the stereotype of the petite and
peaceful poeciliid. Reproduction is via
ovovivipary, with a relatively longer
gestation than other poeciliids.

Belonesox belizanus

Belonesox belizanus

Common Name: pike livebearer
Native Geography: Atlantic coast of
Central America
Biotope: still, vegetated waters,
including brackish
Size: males 4.5 inches (11 cm); females
7 inches (18 cm)
Minimum Tank Size: 36 inches
(90 cm) long
Diet: piscivore; adults will often take
only live fish
Temperature: 76° to 85°F (24° to 29°C)
　　Keep in a single species tank.
Although live blackworms (similar to
tubifex worms but less suspect of
introducing diseases and also easier to
keep alive) and some dry foods have
been reported as substitute fare, feeder
or baby fish need to be the staple diet
of the pike livebearer to maintain good

health and avoid cannibalization in the colony—namely from females and larger male members. Males have a very long gonopodium and perform sneak matings to avoid becoming lunch. Fry can be fed live baby brine shrimp followed a week or two later by fish fry.

The pike livebearer hides among plants, rocks, or tank ornaments waiting to ambush its prey. By contrast, the Yucatan Peninsula race from Mexico *(B. belizanus maxillosus)* will reportedly also hunt in open water. It is this sub-species that was released in south Florida in 1957 and currently preys on native fresh and brackish water fish.

Brachyraphis

A Central American genus currently comprising nine species. While *Brachyraphis* species are beautiful, their popularity is limited by their aggressive and carnivorous manners (which have been known to keep even larger cichlids at bay).

Brachyrhaphis roseni

Common Name: the cardinal brachy
Native Geography: Costa Rica; Panama
Biotope: slow-moving streams and still waters
Size and Sex: males 2 inches (5 cm), females 3 inches (7.5 cm)
Minimum Tank Size: 24 inches (60 cm)
Diet: insectivore; live, frozen, and freeze-dried foods; flakes
Temperature: 67° to 74°F (19° to 23°C)

Keep in a single-species tank. This is the most beautiful species in the genus, but this rose has a thorn, as it is also very aggressive. As a fry eater, few can match the cardinal brachy's skill and appetite for hunting down their own fry. Females will even attack males who are too assertive in their courting. Isolate pregnant females in tanks planted densely with Java moss to protect the fry until their mother can be returned to the main aquarium. Higher temperatures may limit their breeding potential.

Several lovely wild and cultivated forms of *B. roseni* are popular in Europe. Sister species *B. episcopi* and *B. holdridgei* are much more peaceful.

Gambusia

A successful poeciliid genus with over 30 species (some extinct), ranging from the Mid-Atlantic U.S. down to South America. *Belonesox* and *Gambusia* are in the same "tribe" of poeciliids and are noteworthy for being the genera housing the most carnivorous and aggressive species in the family.

Gambusia holbrooki and G. affinis

Gambusia affinis (*pictured here, male left, female right*) and G. holbrook's *are very simliar and often hybridized.*

Common Names: plague
minnow; mosquitofish
Native Geography: *G. affinis:* Indiana
south to Gulf Basin and west to
Mexico; *G. holbrooki:* Atlantic coastal
states from Delaware to Florida
Biotope: varied, from soft to
brackish waters
Size and Sex: females 2.7 inches (7 cm),
males 1.6 inches (4 cm). *G. holbrooki*
is mottled.
Minimum Tank Size: 5 gallons
(20 liters)
Diet: carnivore: carnivore; live, frozen,
and freeze-dried foods; fish fry and
eggs; flakes
Temperature: 50° to 100°F (10° to 38°C)

Mosquitofish are the most widely
distributed fish in the world, due to
its mistaken attribute as primarily a
predator of mosquito larvae. In reality
it is a carnivore that will also prey on
fry (including its own) and on other
fish and their eggs, often resulting in
the eradication of native species and
subsequent ecosystem disruption.
They are often sold in pet shops as
feeder fish and by pond supply outlets
for water gardens.

In the aquarium, *Gambusia affinis*
and *G. holbrooki* are notorious fin
shredders, even attacking fish much
larger than themselves, even picking at
the skin hair on snorkelers! They can
withstand a long water garden season,
but care must be taken that they
do not venture into any local water
bodies! Other *Gambusia* species are
milder and make great aquarium fish.

Girardinus

An old genus of poeciliid, with about
eight members across Cuba's island
system. Characteristic for the genus are
their blue metallic-rimmed eyes.

Girardinus metallicus

Giardinus metallicus, *female above,
male below.*

Common Names: black throat
livebearer; metallic livebearer
Native Geography: Cuba
Biotope: varied; prefers sluggish or
standing waters
Size: males 1.6 inches (4 cm) with
black throat, females 2.7 inches (7 cm)
Minimum Tank Size: 5 gallons (20 liters)
Diet: omnivore; herbivore
Temperature: 65° to 85°F (18° to 29°C)

This old favorite was introduced
at the dawn of the tropical fish hobby
and is probably the best wild-type
livebearer to start with. The current
hobby strain can withstand all kinds of
water conditions. It is marked by the
unique black band that runs through
males extending from their snout all
way down across the gonopodium.
They are also fair algae eaters.

Girardinus metallicus may be a
quasi-annual fish in nature, dying off in
the dry season as their pools evaporate.
At the beginning of the rainy season,

those individuals who survive very quickly repopulate the area with a reported explosion of life. This may explain the extremely fast rate of growth and sexual maturity in the species.

A sister species, *G. falcatus*, is also available in hobby circles and displays particularly interesting courtship and competitive behavior through its use of stalking territories.

Heterandria

A genus of small species ranging from the Mid-Atlantic United States to Central America.

Heterandria formosa

Heterandria formosa

Common Names: mosquito fish; dwarf livebearer, least killifish
Native Geography: Florida, with coastal population north to North Carolina and west to Louisiana along the Gulf Coast
Biotope: weedy or algae-laden waters near the banks
Size: males 0.8 inches (2 cm) with spotted reddish dorsal; females 1.2 inches (3 cm)

Minimum Tank Size: 2.5 gallon (10 liters)
Diet: omnivore; tiny foods
Temperature: 60° to 80°F (16° to 27°C)

A pretty fish, but its size and shyness make it hard to appreciate. Likes to hide near the bottom among large gravel pieces and plants. Great for summer water gardens. A South Carolina population is more golden brown in coloration. It compensates for its tiny size by using superfetation to reproduce, with one to six fry produced every one to four days.

Limia

A popular genus from the Caribbean Islands that makes up about 10 percent of poeciliids. At least 22 species are recognized, with probably more to be discovered on Haiti and Cuba, and some to be merged. At first it was thought that limias were closely related to mollies as a sister genus. Recent DNA sequencing data indicates this is not the case. Evolutionary theories range from a marine migration from the Central/South American land mass about 20 million years ago, to isolation of a poeciliid population when some of the Greater Antilles broke off from the mainland. Limias may be close to ancestral poeciliids.

Limias share a characteristic dorsal spot, at least in their juvenile stage. Many have shimmering scales and contrasting colors that tend to get better with age. Most males mate via sneak copulation with little or no courtship display. But three species do court their females, and are particularly lovely. They do well in calcium-hard or brackish water that is warm and alkaline. Most do just fine in a 10-gallon (40-liter) tank.

Limia nigrofasciata

Limia nigrofasciata

Common Name: humped-backed limia
Native Geography: Haiti
Biotope: well-vegetated fresh and brackish waters
Size: males 2 inches (5 cm) with larger dorsal, females 2.5 inches (6 cm)
Minimum Tank Size: 30 inches (20 gallons) and up (76 cm, 80 liters)
Diet: omnivore; live foods; algae
Temperature: 76° to 82°F (24° to 28°C)

A beautiful and unique fish that displays courtship behavior. The unique shape of the male as it ages and its large rounded dorsal, add to its desirability. Domestic stocks have become touchy charges, prone to ich, lethargy, and intestinal worms. Surprisingly, it does very well in summer water gardens, which may be indicative of a need for a varied diet that includes live foods and algae. Fry are very small and delicate but grow quickly (if not preyed on by

the parents). Make sure to provide calcium-hard water and lots of plants and hiding places. Higher temperatures supposedly produce more males.

On the other side of the island known as Hispaniola is another stunning species that displays courtship behavior, *L. perugiae* from the Dominican Republic. This hardier limia sports a large rounded yellow dorsal fin, shimmering blue sides, and an orange chest.

Limia melanogaster

Limia melanogaster

Common Name: black-bellied limia
Native Geography: Jamaica
Biotope: varied
Size: males and females 2 inch (5 cm)
Minimum Tank Size: 5 gallons (20 liters) and up
Diet: omnivore; algae and vegetable matter
Temperature: 72° to 82°F (22° to 28°C)

A small blue and yellow livebearer that is as active as it is lovely. One of the limias that display courtship behavior. Rare alpha males may have black fins. Domestic stocks are hardier charges that adapt well to a variety of water conditions if they do not change suddenly. Parents generally ignore fry. May be the most ancestral of the described *Limia* species.

Limia vittata

Limia vittata, *male below, female above.*

Common Names: Cuban limia; Dalmatian limia
Native Geography: Cuba
Biotope: well-vegetated fresh and brackish waters
Size: males 2.25 inches (6 cm), females 3.75 inches (10 cm)
Minimum Tank Size: 24 inches (15 gallons) and up (60 cm, 60 liters)
Diet: omnivore
Temperature: 75° to 82°F (24° to 28°C)

A white, almost silvery body is randomly spotted with orange, yellow, and gold markings (especially in alpha males). They are the largest of the limias, with females exhibiting significant girth and incredibly large broods (242 in one recorded birth). Fry are robust and stay near the bottom, as opposed to their parents, who prefer the upper half of the water column. Wild specimens are markedly plain. There is debate about whether the colorful aquarium form of *L. vittata* is the result of hybridization (cross-breeding of different species or races within a species), cultivation (use of selective breeding to enhance a trait), or population (a native geographic form or race).

Poecilia

One of the largest and most successful genus in the family Poeciliidae, with nearly 40 species ranging from North to South America in a variety of waters. Science seems to be moving toward splitting the various sub-genera into their own genera and making *Poecilia* a genus for the short-finned molly-type fish exclusively.

Many *Poecilia* species demonstrate great variability in color and patterns across geographic populations. Consequently, they have been extensively hybridized to create hundreds of varieties of guppies and mollies that have helped popularize the tropical fish hobby since its beginning. The genus does not line-breed well, and strains can weaken after a few generations, making some fancy varieties, especially show fish, delicate charges. Reproduction is generally via ovoviviparity (egg and yolk), though supplemental nourishment from the mother is being discovered in more species.

Poecilia (Lebistes) reticulata

A fancy form of Poecilia reticulata, *the popular and beautiful guppy.*

Endler's livebearer.

Common Name: guppy
Native Geography: northern South America (above the Amazon) and surrounding islands
Biotope: variety of calm waters
Size: males 1 inch (2.5 cm), females 2 inches (5 cm). Fancy guppies are larger-bodied and larger-tailed than their wild cousins.
Minimum Tank Size: 2.5 gallons and up (10 liters)
Diet: omnivorous; relishes small water crustaceans and insect larvae
Temperature: 68° to 82°F (20° to 28°C)

With the possible exception of the goldfish, the guppy is the most popular hobbyist fish in the world, with many color and finnage varieties. Its natural variability is primarily an adaptation to predator co-habitation. Guppies continue to be a source of scientific investigation as well, with recent findings suggesting that individual members of a colony have personalities (e.g., risk-taking) as well as an elaborate communication system to warn of predators.

Guppies are a perfect colorful and lively pet for a small desktop aquarium to a large show tank. As a coastal South American species, the guppy tolerates a range of water chemistries (including soft acidic water) better than most other livebearers. But it is not as temperature-tolerant as Central American species. Wild-type guppies are sold as feeder fish in many stores and are particularly hardy, but feeder tanks can harbor disease, so observe carefully. Most hobbyists opt for fancy guppies, which are so radically different from the wild forms that they are hardly recognizable as the same species. Championship strains rival marine fish in beauty and "wow" effect, but pet shop strains are hardier. The most spectacular wild race is the metallic-hued "Endler's livebearer" from Venezuela. Anatomical, behavioral, and DNA analyses reveals it is not an independent species as often noted. Proposed species status as "*P. wingei*" may be due in part to conservation efforts. Hobby strains are nearly all hybrids with other guppy populations.

Poecilia (Mollienesia) sphenops

A typical "sphenops" molly, with a lot of P. sphenops *ancestry.*

Common Name: short-finned molly
Native Geography: North America, primarily Mexico
Biotope: variety of waters; especially creeks
Size: males 2 inches (5 cm) and slimmer, females 3 inches (7.5 cm)
Minimum Tank Size: 20 gallons (80 liters)
Diet: omnivorous; algae; vegetable
Temperature: wild-types 70° to 82°F (21° to 28°C); fancy hybrids 77° to 86°F (25° to 30°C)

This species name is often incorrectly applied to the "gold dust," "balloon," "black," and other small mollies sold in pet shops. In reality they are all hybrids of various molly species, selectively bred since the 1920s. Black mollies are particularly delicate and do best at high temperatures near or over 80°F (27°C), with high-quality calcium-hard water.

In the wild there are many races of *P. sphenops* with different colors, fin patterns, and sizes. Characteristic of all are horizontal rows of small dots on its flanks. They also display an alpha male pecking order, and fry should be offered some protection through heavy top and bottom plantings.

Scientifically, *P. sphenops* has become a "dump" category for just about any undescribed short-finned molly. Its range was once reported as more widespread. Most recently the non-Mexican races known as the liberty mollies, with their red-banded or reticulated dorsal fins, were split out as *P. salvatoris*. Here, too, hobby stocks are likely hybrids.

Poecilia (Mollienesia) velifera

A sailfin molly, Poecilia velifera *type.*

Common Names: giant sailfin molly; Yucatan molly
Native Geography: northern half of the Yucatan Peninsula
Biotope: algae-laden coastal still waters
Size: males 5 inches (13 cm), females 6 inches (16 cm). Males possess giant dorsal fin and more color.
Minimum Tank Size: 30 inches (76 cm)
Diet: omnivorous; algae; herbivore
Temperature: wild-types 72° to 82°F (22° to 28°C); fancy hybrids 77° to 86°F (25° to 30°C)

How Could I Forget the Coolest Livebearer?

Have you ever wished you could magically make a copy of yourself? Well, this fish can!

Hailing from the region of the Rio Grande, *Poecilia formosa* appears to be just an unremarkable short-finned molly. In reality, it is a remarkable fish because it is an all-female species of livebearer!

Discovered in 1932, *P. formosa*, the Amazon molly, is a "sexual predator," enticing males from other molly species residing in its habitat to mate. But these males do not contribute a set of chromosomes in union with a set from a female egg to create a fish, as is commonly done across life forms. Instead, the sperm from these males simply activates a "cloning" process for the female eggs, which already possess a set of paired chromosomes (a diploid zygote). The males do not contribute to the heredity of the offspring. All the resulting fry are females and duplicates of their mother as well as the founding member of the species!

Rarely, a "triploid" fish will emerge in a batch of fry, which is a hybrid between *P. formosa* and the host male. It possesses one-half more chromosomes than either parent fish: the full/diploid set from the *P. formosa* egg plus the half/haploid set from the male sperm cell. Another anomaly occurs when crossing Amazon mollies with pet shop black mollies. Some of these fry have black spotting, even though they are still cloned diploid fish from the Amazon molly eggs. The spotting does not carry through future generations, indicating that some invasion of genetic material is restructuring the genetic coding of the embryos.

The native species is the most spectacular member of the sailfin complex of mollies, which includes the similar *P. latipinna* from Mexico and the southern U.S., and *P. petenensis* from Mexico. Males create a spectacular visual display, erecting their giant dorsal fin to entice females. Pet shop strains are hybrids with other mollies, arguably the most delicate of the common livebearers. Wild-types tend to be hardier and endure lower temperatures.

In the wild, many sailfin mollies are found in brackish waters near the coast, which can be simulated with a 50-50 mix of fresh and synthetic sea water, for a specific gravity of about 1.012 (regular monitoring of tank water with a hydrometer is recommended). Professional breeders do not generally use salt, however, as salt will curb or eliminate the use of vegetative filtration. Success has been found with (1) calcium-rich water in the upper hardness range, (2) varied filtration to eliminate all ammonia, (3) higher temperatures, (4) low stocking density, and (5) frequent water changes.

Other Poecilia Species

P. mexicana (Central America, Mexico): An ancestral species, also with many races and sub-species. A cave form with poor eyesight also exists. Males of a Mexican population were discovered to set up territories in algae pits to lure females for mating.

P. chica (Mexico): The peaceful dwarf molly relishes algae and plant matter in its diet. It tolerates a wide range of water conditions.

P. vivipara (South America): The one-spot livebearer is a variable species found in a variety of waters. Brackish water can change its appearance.

Poecilia vivipara

P. caucana (Pacific Central America and northern South America): Sports a snappy yellow/black dorsal; now popular on the auction circuit. Often found in algae-laden brackish water. Fry can be preyed on by the parents.

Poeciliopsis

Known collectively as the "top minnows" because of their torpedo shape and surface-dwelling tendencies.

The *Poeciliopsis* species number about 20 (possibly more) species that range from as far north as the American Southwest all the way down to Colombia, South America. *P. occidentalis* from Arizona is now critically endangered because of a *Gambusia* introduction into its home waters.

Reproduction varies from ovoviviparity (*P. monacha*) to possibly true viviparity (*P. prolifica*). Superfetation is employed as well. All-female races exist within populations of *P. lucida* and *P. occidentalis*, both of which use the sperm from male *P. lucida, P. occidentalis,* and *P .infans* to stimulate the development of their eggs.

Poeciliopsis gracilis

Poeciliopsis gracilis

Common Name: porthole livebearer
Native Geography: large range from the Atlantic to Pacific sides of Mexico, Honduras, and Guatemala
Biotope: planted areas of streams
Size: males 1.5 inches (4 cm), females 2 inches (5 cm). Males are slimmer.
Minimum Tank Size: 10 gallons (40 liters)
Diet: omnivorous; vegetable

Temperature: 75° to 85°F (24° to 29°C)

The porthole livebearer is a delightful little species that reminds the hobbyist of a leopard danio in appearance and behavior. The hobby population is silvery blue with a row of purple spots on its flanks and some gold in its finnage. Males are "thruster"-type maters, usually sneaking up from behind a female. A batch of fry are born about every ten days. They are easy to spot, displaying the same coloration as their parents. Juveniles are shy compared to adults.

The porthole livebearer benefits from clean water and higher temperatures. Regional varieties exist, with those outside Mexico possibly being *P. pleurospilus*. A population in California's polluted Salton Sea was accidentally introduced in the 1970s.

Xiphophorus

The genus that houses the popular platies and swordtails. Comprising at least 23 species, it is divided into three clades: the northern swordtails, the southern swordtails, and the platies. They are varied in color, pattern, and finnage across different populations. Because they will interbreed, a myriad of colorful varieties has been developed for the hobby. Commercially available fish are adaptable and hardy.

Xiphophorus evolved relatively recently, about 1 million years ago. *Xiphophorus* species' biological responses to behavioral and social cues are fascinating. Much of the genus displays extreme leap fish phenomena (see Chapter 1) with sexual maturation taking over a year in some species, and males anatomically disguising themselves as females in the presence of an alpha male. Species utilize a host of biological communications, including chemical signals in their urine, UV light reflection and perception, color, and long caudal fin extensions (the sword tail), to attract mates and prevent hybridization with other species.

Xiphophorus genetics are equally complex. Since most platies and swords can be line bred for generations, a consistent and reliable gene pool is readily available. Consequently, they are utilized in animal models to study cancer inheritance, genetics, and pollution effects. This also makes them a perfect fish for beginners, breeders, and farmers alike.

Reproduction is via ovoviviparity (egg and yolk), though supplemental nourishment from the mother has been observed in several species. Most are good algae eaters.

Xiphophorus maculatus

A red platy, aquarium strain of hybrid origin.

Common Names: platy, moon
Native Geography: from the Atlantic

slope of southern Mexico through Guatemala, Belize, and Honduras
Biotope: springs and a variety of still waters or banks; often shallow and vegetated
Size: 2 inches (5 cm) but usually smaller; wild males smaller than females
Minimum Tank Size: 5 gallons (20 liters) and up
Diet: omnivore; algae
Temperature: 65° to 85°F (18° to 29°C)

Peaceful, lively, and hardy, platies are the perfect small aquarium fish and the best livebearer for beginners. They are available in an endless variety of colors, patterns, and finnage, with trade names such as "wagtail," "sunburst," and "calico," among others. In reality all fancy platies should be considered hybrids of various *Xiphophorus* species, selectively bred since the start of the tropical fish hobby. Wild species and red platies are more delicate and do better at higher temperatures.

The platy is probably the most polymorphic vertebrate on our planet (varied colors and patterns within and among populations). Some races have a gene that suppresses their black spotting. In hybrid crosses with unspotted swordtails, some offspring develop melanomas. This finding established a genetic link to cancer. They are also the only vertebrate in which both males and females have multiple sex chromosomes. There can be two kinds of males (XY, YY) and three kinds of females (XX, WX, WY) among platies. Their colors, finnage, and body patterns are linked

to their sex typing, making them more challenging to breed selectively than even guppies.

Xiphophorus hellerii

A *wild-type swordtail, perhaps pure* Xiphophorus hellerii.

Common Name: swordtail
Native Geography: from the Atlantic slope of southern Mexico through Guatemala, Belize, and Honduras
Biotope: diverse waters
Size: males up to 9 inches (23 cm) including sword; females 5 inches (13 cm). Pet shop strains smaller—much smaller in most cases.
Minimum Tank Size: 24 inches (60 cm) long
Diet: omnivore; carnivore
Temperature: 68° to 82°F (20° to 28°C)

As with platies, pet shop and fancy strains are hybrids of various *Xiphophorus* species. Most are hardy; "red velvets," though, are more delicate and do better at higher temperatures. After years of selecting the males with the biggest swords on the farm for sale (and leaving the smaller fish to continue breeding), the commercially bred swordtail of today is a short-sworded shadow of its former glory.

In the wild, so many regional

varieties exist, including those with differing behaviors, that future splitting of the species may occur. *X. alvarezi* and *X. clemenciae* are two examples of *hellerii*-like species. Some populations reveal no obvious sex chromosomes, and sex might be determined by a combination of genetic "switches" determined by social structure and/or inheritance.

Male swordtails can be aggressive towards each other, making it difficult to house more than one developed male in a tank. The male's gonopodium sports an elaborate mix of bony and fleshy hooks and clasps, resulting in seconds of attached swimming with the female. The sword-like tail aids the male in swimming backwards during courting.

Xiphophorus variatus

A variatus platy.

Common Name: variatus; variatus platy; platy variatus
Native Geography: broad range on the Atlantic slope of southern Mexico
Biotope: variety of quiet backwaters, often vegetated and algae-laden
Size: males 2.25 inches (6 cm) and more colorful; females 2.5 inches (6 cm)
Minimum Tank Size: 5 gallons (20 liters) and up
Diet: omnivore; herbivore; algae
Temperature: wild-types 60° to 85°F (16° to 29°C)

A unique *Xiphophorus* color-wise, *X. variatus* displays "variation" within and among geographic populations. This extends to their temperature tolerance as well, making them great residents for a long season of water gardening or an unheated aquarium. This is particularly true of descendants of the Rio Axtla populations ("blue parrot") which are seasonally available at pet store chains. The spectacular colors of the males can take a year or more to develop, often reaching their maximum intensity in the last months of life, and more so with an alpha male. Most other fish in the colony will resemble females if raised from juveniles, thereby protecting themselves from aggression.

More common in stores are the consistently colorful hybrids, such as "Hawaiian" and "canary yellow." Variatus have a wide dorsal and can support a hifin trait better than most other platies and swordtails. Their body shape lies somewhere between a platy and a swordtail.

Selecting Fancy Livebearers

Before purchasing fancy livebearers, make sure to find out the temperature and water conditions from the breeder and try to duplicate these conditions. Then gradually over a month get the fish used to your aquarium conditions. Their progeny will adapt even easier.

If there is a particular strain of fancy livebearer that suits your eye, and you want to maintain the strain, make sure you obtain fish of the same variety. This is not a problem when purchasing show-quality livebearers, as strains are always separated. These fish can rival marine species in color and beauty.

The drawback to show-quality livebearers is that they are often raised in nearly sterile conditions, with daily water changes and live food in bare tanks. Subsequently, they often do not develop the immunity or hardiness of fish store and feral varieties (*Xiphophorus* are the exception here). But they usually adjust if you practice good basic aquarium maintenance.

Xiphophorus montezumae

Xiphophorus montezumae

Common Names: Montezuma sword; giant swordtail
Native Geography: Mexico
Biotope: clear waters near springs, rivers, and falls
Size: males up to 10 inches (25 cm) including sword; females 2.5 inches (6 cm)
Minimum Tank Size: 20-gallon (80-liter) "high"
Diet: omnivore; live foods
Temperature: 70° to 78°F (21° to 26°C)

A great show fish whose sword length is the stuff of legend. All the males have the characteristic sword tail that can be up to three times the body length, as well as a large rounded dorsal. Males can take one to two years to sex out, confusing hobbyists in thinking they have a tankful of female fish. While the 20-gallon long works for most, in my experience this long-tailed species, like most wild swordtails, does best in larger tanks.

Xiphophorus birchmanni

Xiphophorus birchmanni

Common Names: sheepshead swordtail; swordless swordtail
Native Geography: Hidalgo, Mexico in the Rio Panuco Drainage
Biotope: flowing, rocky waters, some quite fast
Size: 2.5 inches (6 cm) males have a large dorsal and vertical body striping
Minimum Tank Size: 24 inches (60 cm) long
Diet: omnivore; live foods
Temperature: 70° to 75°F (21° to 24°C)

This Northern Mountain swordtail has made quite a splash at recent livebearer shows and scientific venues. The male's large yellow finnage and humped head and back more than make up for its tiny sword (if any). As you would guess from its biotope, the sheepshead swordtail does best in highly oxygenated water. It is a shy fish that does best in a colony.

Although the fish sports a large dorsal, it was discovered that unlike as in mollies, this finnage is not used to entice females but to ward off competing suitors (females actually prefer smaller dorsals). Also, it was later discovered that a male will spray his urine in the direction of a female to entice mating and to distinguish himself from *X. malinche* and *X. cortezi*, who inhabit different parts of its range. Sadly, pollution in its biotope is disrupting this chemical communication system and creating hybrid fish.

Other Xiphophorus *Species*
X. nigrensis: A pygmy swordtail with different size classes, and UV light reflection and perception to attract mates.

X. couchianus: An extinct-in-nature platy that does best in a large colony with floating and bottom planting.

X. nezahualcoyotl: "Nezzies" are livebearer fan favorites with their curved swords and spotted bodies.

Xiphophorus nigrensis

Family Goodeidae
The livebearing goodeids (or splitfins) are an interesting group of about 40 species native to west-central Mexico's highland plateau, in and around the Rio Lerma Basin. They are an old fish family, with fossil records going back about 25 million years. Goodeids probably evolved from a *Profundulus*-like killifish ancestor. But they were generally unknown to the hobby, and to many scientists, until the 1970s. Most of the hobby stocks trace their roots back to the collection of American aquarist James K. Langhammer, who has been selflessly giving them away since the late 1960s. While curator of the Belle Isle Aquarium, he obtained transfers from Dr. Robert Rush Miller, who was describing the family for science and foresaw the environmental peril in Mexico.

Common Finnage Varieties in Livebearers

Lyretail*: Extended dorsal and caudal finnage also affects the males' gonopodiums, making them unable to mate with females.

Hifin*: Extended dorsal, mostly seen in fancy *Xiphophorus*.

Sailfin: A naturally high fin, such as seen in some mollies.

Delta Tail*: A guppy caudal fin that is shaped like a large triangle. Very popular among guppy breeders in the U. S.

Pin (Plume) Tail*: An extension in the middle of the caudal fin that comes to a point. Often seen in fancy platies.

Brush Tail*: The entire caudal fin is extended. Mostly seen in fancy *Xiphophorus*.

Swordtail: The lower part of the caudal fin extends outward like a sword. Natural in many *Xiphophorus* species and some guppies.

Double Sword: The upper and lower parts of the caudal fin are both extended. Common in some fancy guppies.

*traits are mutations fixed in domesticated strains

Male goodeids do not sport the complex gonopodium structure of the poeciliids for inseminating females. Instead, the flexible part of the front of the anal fin is separated by a notch and known as an andropodium. Mating takes longer, and cooperation from the female is required. This single characteristic leads to an interesting mix of social behaviors.

Female goodeids cannot store sperm like poeciliids. A new mating is needed for every pregnancy, which lasts about twice as long (60 days). They are truly viviparous in their reproduction. Goodeid females (except maybe *Ataeniobius toweri*) nourish their young with umbilical cord-like structures called trophotaeniae. The fry are born in smaller numbers, but with remarkably larger size and fuller form than poeciliid fry. Witnessing the birth of a goodeid is something every hobbyist should make an effort to behold at least once.

With few exceptions, goodeids are best considered cool-water tropicals. Because of the 3,000- to 7,000-foot (up to 2-km) elevations on the Mexican plateau, goodeids have evolved in extremes in temperature, both seasonally and daily. Temperature fluctuations of 35 degrees Fahrenheit in a 24-hour period are common, and a nightly frost after a day of hot sun can occur at higher altitudes. Subsequently, most goodeids are healthier when kept at temperatures that fluctuate seasonally from 60° to 70°F in (16° to 21°C) winter and 70° to 80°F (21° to 27°C) in the summer—unheated aquariums, tanks at the lower rack in a fishroom, summer water gardens. Breeding is more productive and extends for more years when these seasonal temperature changes are simulated.

Goodeids are an exquisite example of adaptive radiation. They range in size from 2 to 12 inches (5 to 30 cm). There are the long and fast *Ilyodon* from moving waters to the stocky sail-finned *Skiffia* from quiet backwaters. Thanks to the Internet, goodeids are more popular than ever. But nearly all are endangered, with some already extinct or on the brink, because of pollution and water usage that may have already destroyed up to 80 percent of their natural habitat. Combined with their less fecund nature, goodeids are ideal candidates for species maintenance by hobbyists.

Characodon

The most northerly of the Mexican goodeids, and also the most colorful. The taxonomy of the genus is currently in flux, and location and collection names should be used until true species can be assigned.

Characodon sp. "lateralis" (Los Beros)

Characodon sp. *"lateralis"*

Common Name: rainbow goodeid
Native Geography: Durango, Mexico
Biotope: quiet vegetated waters and springs; marshes
Size: males 1.75 inches (4 cm), females 2.25 inches (6 cm)
Minimum Tank Size: 10 gallons (40 liters) and up
Diet: omnivore; live foods; vegetable and algae matter
Temperature: 67° to 76°F (19° to 24°C)

Males display sparkles of blue, yellow, green, and brown against a swatch of red. The mating ritual is interesting, and parents rarely touch their fry. The fry are especially large, even for goodeids. Provide plenty of cover, as males can be aggressive towards each other (and outnumber females in a brood). A shy species when not feeding. Acclimate them very slowly, especially when coming inside from a summer water garden. A similar species (race?) is *C. audax*, known as the black prince because of its finnage color. They are all well worth the effort and make great show fish.

Skiffia

A small, compact genus referred to as the sawfin goodeids because of the irregular spiky dorsal fin on the males. Skiffias tolerate extended high temperatures better than most other goodeids.

Skiffia multipunctata

Skiffia multipunctata

Common Names: spotted skiffia; piebald skiffia
Native Geography: Guadalajara, Mexico
Biotope: variety of quiet waters
Size: males 2 inches (5 cm) with elaborate dorsal, females 2.3 inches (6 cm)
Minimum Tank Size: 10 gallons (40 liters) and up
Diet: omnivore
Temperature: 63° to 78°F (17° to 26°C)

A variable species that is peaceful and hardy. Piebald morphs make good show fish. A fertile hybrid called the black beauty was developed by US-livebearer pioneer James K. Langhammer by crossing *S. multipunctata* with the now extinct-in-nature *S. francesae. S. lermae* and *S. bilineata* (the first goodeid introduced to the hobby back in the 1930s) are other good skiffias to try, albeit less dramatic in coloration.

Ilyodon

These are long, streamlined fish known as the bass goodeids.

Ilyodon furcidens "xantusi"

Ilyodon furcidens "xanusi"

Common Names: the xantusi; bass goodeid
Native Geography: Colima, Mexico
Biotope: pools or swift water in highland rivers and streams, Mexico
Size: males 3.75 inches (10 cm) with more color; females 4 inches (10 cm)
Minimum Tank Size: 30 inches (75 cm) length
Diet: omnivore; algae
Temperature: 64° to 79°F (18° to 26°C)

An extremely active but not particularly intelligent species, with beautiful yellow and blue coloring. Reminds one of a giant danio. A ravenous appetite, it will eat (or try to eat) nearly anything. Older males develop a slight hump. They are very hardy and make good dither fish (fish added to ease other specimens' nervousness) for cooler cichlid tanks.

I. furcidens appears to be in the midst of evolving to two species, with a

Be a Responsible Fish Owner

Never mix pure species from the same genus in an aquarium, or hybridization could occur. If you work with a hybrid, label it as so when sharing the fish or its progeny.

Never release unwanted aquarium fish, plants, or amphibians into local bodies of water. Many ecosystems and native species have been severely and permanently disrupted because of this practice. Every aquatic organism has evolved to live together *in*, and thus *create*, a unique biotope. Don't disrupt this delicate balance in the cycle of life!

wide-mouth form (*I. furcidens xantusi*) and a narrow-mouth form (*I. furcidens furcidens*) adapting to different feeding niches in the same biotope.

Ameca

A single-species genus and the first goodeid to gain hobby popularity in the early 1970s. Its atypical tolerance for warm or polluted water makes it a good beginner goodeid. Hobby stocks are completely domesticated and very forgiving, so the genus is highly recommended.

Ameca splendens

Ameca splendens

Common Name: butterfly goodeid
Native Geography: Mexico in the Rio Ameca and its tributary, Rio Teuchitlan
Biotope: shallow stretches of the river, often with vegetation.
Size: males 3.2 inches (8 cm) with more color; females 4.5 inches (11 cm) with spotted horizontal body striping
Minimum Tank Size: 30 inches (76 cm) length
Diet: omnivore; herbivore
Temperature: 65° to 85°F (18° to 29°C)

A very hardy fish with older and alpha males sporting various metallic shades of blue, green, and yellow on their scales, and a yellow-edged caudal fin. Its color, lively behavior, and size make for a good show fish. Surprisingly, female butterflies begin the courtship ritual by quivering in front of the male. Males form a pecking order and can be aggressive to each other.

Xenotoca

Comprises three species of compact but colorful goodeids.

Xenotoca eiseni

Xenotoca eiseni

Common Name: red-tailed goodeid
Native Geography: broad range on
Mexico's west-central Pacific slope
Biotope: varied
Size: males 2 inches (5 cm) with more
color; females 2.75 inches (7 cm) with
faint body striping
Minimum Tank Size: 5 gallons
(20 liters)
Diet: omnivore
Temperature: 60° to 79°F (16° to 26°C)
   Males of some populations have a
unique bluish band in the back half
of the body, adjacent to the red tail.
Different color morphs exist, both
in nature (e.g., "San Marcos") and
through years of selective breeding.
A remarkably hardy fish in nature, it
was one of the early hobby goodeids
and is now fully domesticated. Reports
of fin-nipping other fish are mixed,
and seems to occur in line-bred
populations. They will breed at a very
small size, and if kept in the low 70s
(about 21° to 23°C), nearly year-round.

Zoogoneticus

Comprises two species of currently
popular goodeids.

Zoogoneticus tequila

Zoogoneticus tequila

Common Names: the tequila; the
crescent zoe
Native Geography: Rio Teuchitlan,
Mexico
Biotope: shallow still waters
Size: males 2.5 inches (6 cm) with
yellow tail crescent; females 3 inches
(7.5 cm)
Minimum Tank Size: 10 gallons
(40 liters)
Diet: omnivore
Temperature: 65° to 75°F (18° to 24°C)
   The male tequila sports shimmering
scales and a unique iridescent yellow-
orange crescent on its tail, with a
body that becomes almost black when
mating. Larger and more aggressive
alpha males can emerge. It is now
extinct in nature with its cohabiter,
Skiffia francesae. Hobby stocks are
progeny from the original discovery.
Its genetics have been complex
enough to sustain the line over its
years in captivity.

Family Anablepidae

This is the smallest of our four
livebearing families, and it comprises
three oddball species. They are spread
out from Central to South America.

The male copulatory organ is tubular, allowing a more directed flow of sperm. The family consists of five species across three genera.

Anableps

The famed four-eyed fish. These elongated surface swimmers have a split field of vision. The eyes of *Anableps* are asymmetrical and can focus on objects above and below the waterline at the same time. The eyes are thicker and more curved below water, and thinner and less curved above the water. This adaptation is due to the different way light is refracted (bent) under water, as well as being less available, compared to atmospheric sunlight. All three species in this genus are primarily brackish-water fish.

Anableps anableps

Anableps anableps

Common Name: the four-eyed fish
Native Geography: central to northern South America
Biotope: mud flats and mangrove swamps, very shallow waters
Size: 10 inches (30 cm)
Minimum Tank Size: 48 inches (120 cm) in length

Diet: carnivore; krill; fruit flies
Temperature: 80° to 89°F (27° to 32°C)

A specialized setup is advised. *A. anableps* is a surface swimmer, so depth is relatively unimportant. Floating plastic plants or ornaments, or platforms that reach just below the surface, will provide basking areas where the fish can haul themselves out of the water (absolutely necessary for developing fry). A well-covered tank is needed to keep the air moist, reduce heat dissipation, and hold back these adequate jumpers. Create brackish conditions using a 50-50 mix of fresh and synthetic sea water, for a specific gravity of about 1.012 (regular monitoring of tank water with a hydrometer is recommended).

SMALL FRY

Where to Start?

The most commonly available livebearers you and your children will find in pet stores are fancy guppies, mollies, platies, and swordtails. Each comes in seemingly endless colors and finnage varieties. Guppies, platies, and swordtails are easy to care for and are a good choice for the first aquarium. Mollies, on the other hand, are best reserved for later.

Stillbirths are not uncommon in stressed females. Feeding krill appears to aid in their well-being.

Family Hemirhamphidae

This varied family of at least 110 species includes both livebearing and egglaying fishes, occupying soft fresh waters and marine and brackish biotopes. They are known as the halfbeaks because of their longer or more elaborate lower jaw. Three livebearing genera have been kept by hobbyists: *Dermogenys, Hemirhamphodon*, and *Nomorhamphus*. Males possess a well-formed andropodium, which means courtship and female cooperation is necessary for sperm transfer. The aquarium can be shallow with a tight cover, as these fish are surface dwellers. Their fry are large, but these are carnivorous fish, and the fry should be separated from their parents immediately.

Dermogenys pusilla

Dermogenys pusilla

Common Name: wrestling halfbeak
Native Geography: broad range across Southeast Asia
Biotope: fresh and brackish shallow waters

Size: 3 inches (7.5 cm)
Minimum Tank Size: 24 inches (60 cm)
Diet: carnivore; fruit flies; floating freeze-dried and flakes
Temperature: 68° to 86°F (20° to 30°C)

A wonderful small halfbeak that is now domesticated and quite adaptable. Males may fight, but real danger comes from skittish fish running into the tank glass and damaging their "beaks." A few pieces of floating hornwort or other live or plastic plant calm the fish, where it forms mini-territories, sometimes in pairs. In nature many populations or sub-species exist that vary by color and water requirements.

Nomorhamphus liemi

Common Names: Celebes halfbeak;

Nomorhamphus liemi

bearded halfbeak; beakless halfbeak
Native Geography: southern Sulawesi (Celebes)
Biotope: cooler highland waters; flowing and still waters
Size: males 2.75 inches (7 cm) reddish with fleshly lobe on lower jaw; females 3.5 inches (9 cm)
Minimum Tank Size: 24 inches (60 cm)
Diet: carnivore; live and freeze-dried foods; flakes
Temperature: 68° to 76°F (20° to 24°C)

Males are unique-looking for freshwater fish and display to females continually. They are also extremely competitive among themselves, and occasional fights with mortal injuries have been reported. Water that is soft/acidic to slight hard/alkaline is recommended. *N. liemi liemi* and *N. liemi snijdersi* are the two sub-species.

Red wagtail platies, a great livebearer for beginners.

Chapter 8

What's Next?

At this point in your reading, you may have decided *which* livebearers you want to try, *how* you want to keep them, and *what* equipment and techniques you will use to keep them healthy. There is also a good chance that you already are keeping and breeding livebearers, enjoy reading about them, and just want to take your hobby to another level. There are many ways to further explore the livebearer hobby while making some friends along the way.

Phalloceros caudimaculatus, *a wild-type livebearer.*

This chapter is designed to open up the *organized* livebearer hobby to you, something that has never been covered by a separate chapter dedicated to that topic in any previously published book. Livebearer hobbyists are well regarded in aquarium circles as some of the friendliest and most sociable people in the aquarium hobby. Through this network, you can enjoy fishy fellowship, acquire hard-to-find species, competitively show your animals, and find an outlet to sell or trade your surplus stock.

Aquarium Clubs

The concept of the modern fish club or aquarium society dates back to the 1800s. The aquarium hobby was already popular in North America, thanks to hobbyist/dealer/publisher Hugo Mullertt, and the public and private aquariums that sprang up via P.T. Barnum and others. Never before had the average person been able to peer into the wonders of the underwater world so clearly without getting wet! But the expense of equipment resulting from a lack of mass production, and the complexities caused by a lack of electricity, made the home aquarium a pastime mostly for the well-to-do and men of leisure. The focus at this time was on coldwater species like goldfish and native fish.

Towards the end of the nineteenth century, German hobbyists (pioneers in tropical fish importation and husbandry) emigrated to the United States and began meeting informally in groups in New York and other large eastern cities to discuss breeding and acquiring fish. Around the turn of the century, formal aquarium societies became established via scientific and hobbyist connections. Goldfish shows and breeding circles were popular.

In the first decade of the twentieth century, tropical or exotic fish as they were called starting making their debut and quickly overtook native fish and goldfish as the "in" species. Livebearers made their debut as early pioneers, imported by a New York City customs agent and hobbyist, Richard Dorn, of

New Jersey. These included platies and swordtails (which were soon discovered to interbreed), guppies, Floridian mollies, and a few wild-type livebearers such as *Phalloceros caudimaculatus*.

The modern-day aquarium club or society is very different from these early incarnations, but they still offer the same things to the hobbyist. At their heart they are non-profit, informal social organizations where you can mingle with other fishheads and make new friends. They usually meet once a month at a meeting hall or nature center, where they serve up light refreshments, an informative guest speaker with colorful slides, door prizes and raffles using donations from aquarium product manufacturers, and a mini-auction of members' surplus fish and breeding output.

As mentioned earlier in this book, fish club auctions are a great way to acquire those livebearers you just won't find in stores, fish that only circulate among hardcore hobbyists. Many of the auction fish (and plants) come from the club's Breeders Award Program. This is another great aspect of the club scene, where your growing achievements as a fish breeder can be recognized by your peers.

Many fish clubs also host monthly bowl shows, annual all-species shows, and weekend workshops with speakers and an award banquet. Throughout the year "shop hops" or other day trips such as local collecting or public aquarium outings are enjoyed. A monthly club newsletter with informative articles is standard. All in all, the low membership fees these clubs charge are well worth the expense!

Most aquarium societies are freshwater generalist in nature, but there are a few livebearer clubs as well. Most are geared towards the fancy-guppy hobby, but a few have emerged that are livebearer specialty clubs. There are also two national livebearer hobby organizations—the American Livebearer Association (ALA) and the International Fancy Guppy Association (IFGA)—that provide their members a monthly journal, trading post, and an annual convention where breeders from around the world converge to show, sell, and swap species and stories.

Together Time

Maintaining an aquarium with your kids is a great family activity. Bonds will strengthen, laughs will be shared, and knowledge will be imparted. What more could you ask for?

Online Aquarium Websites and Forums

Aquarium hobbyists were some of the first users of the Internet—initially as dial-up newsgroups, later to bulletin boards of subscription services such as Compuserve's FISHNET, and now to websites and message forums across the World Wide Web. There are so many aquarium sites and forums, actually, that it is difficult to know where to go and what information you can trust.

There are no editorial boards for aquarium websites and no technical editors for message forums. To be truthful, lots of bad and inaccurate information about livebearers and the aquarium hobby can be found on the Internet, even on sites that appear official or professional. As a hobbyist, you must be able to filter out the style

from the substance. This is why a book like the one you are reading is essential. Remember: anyone can create a website or post to a web forum or blog!

However, Internet aquarium forums and blogs provide a way to chat to other hobbyists, via email or message boards on the site. While not a substitute for a live aquarium club, they are a convenient way to exchange information and tips, as well as sometimes being the only way to meet fellow livebearer hobbyists when a live club is not convenient to you. You can also converse with people around the world in places you will never visit.

When looking for livebearer information and message forums on the web, your first stop should be the national livebearer aquarium societies, such as the ALA or BLA (British Livebearer Association), and

Aquarium clubs will hold auctions where you can obtain new species that interest you.

The fancy guppy is usually the species that draws people to livebearing fish. However, there are so many more beautiful species out there. All you have to do is look.

the IFGA. The information on these sites has been vetted or written by experienced hobbyists. They also have message boards you can browse or participate in. These sites can also provide links they deem worthy of your consideration.

The Show Circuit

No other aquarium specialty offers more of a chance to show your stuff than the livebearer hobby. Many clubs serve up an annual fish show, replete with judges and awards. These shows usually occur in the fall after the summer grow-out season; they feature multiple classes for different kinds of fish—and different kinds of livebearers.

National organizations like the ALA hold shows at their annual conventions that attract entries and hobbyists from all over the world. Guppy organizations like the IFGA sanction shows year-round at various local guppy clubs around the country. These tend to be the most competitive of the livebearer shows in terms of the quality of the fish—but not in terms of the temperament of the contestants (livebearer hobbyists are a friendly lot).

Do not be intimidated. Nearly every show I have attended has been highlighted by a novice hobbyist who took home a first-, second-, or third-place prize with a fish they just took good care of in their aquarium. This is because many factors go into what makes a winning fish, and not all fish cooperate with these standards after they are transported to the showroom! This has been especially evident in recent years at guppy shows, where years of inbreeding and near-sterile rearing conditions by breeders have resulted in fish that do not acclimate well to new water conditions. It is always a good idea to bring some of your own conditioned tap water to the show for your fish, as well as some ammonia neutralizer, as the show tanks are usually unfiltered.

There is great satisfaction and feedback obtained from showing your fish. Judges are usually trained or have years of experience in evaluating fish. The best-looking livebearers are found at shows, so it is also a source for inspiration and future breeding endeavors. Friendships and trading partners are made at such events, and most shows end with an auction during which you can obtain hard-to-find species and strains. So go for it and show your fish! If not for a prize, then for the experience.

Selling Your Fish

The fecundity of many livebearers can lead to lots of unwanted fish in just a few months, especially if raised separately. Sometimes this is intentional if you have a species or strain that is rare or much in demand. In the 1990s the mysterious guppy strain known as Endler's livebearer, followed by the giant-sworded

Xiphophorus montezumae, created boom and bust cycles for buyers and sellers.

Because of this, do not plan to get rich selling your livebearers. Breed fish you enjoy or that interest you, and if some extra money comes along, then you are helping to support your hobby.

Independent pet stores are always interested in good fancy livebearers that are healthy, especially hifin and lyretail swords and platies; delta-tail guppies; and sailfin mollies. These strains often do not ship well, so a local source for healthy stock is appreciated by both the shop's owner and customers.

When selling fish to stores, make sure they are of adult size. These will earn you the top dollar and will more likely win you a steady customer in the shop owner.

Another avenue for selling your fish is the aquarium club auction as mentioned previously. Prices here may be the same or higher than selling to shops, but you usually share 30 to 50 percent of your profits with the club.

Xiphophours montezumae *with very long tails are always in demand.*

The exciting world of livebearers awaits you!

You can also sell smaller fish here that would not be suitable for a retail store. Auctions are a primary funding source for these essential hobby organizations.

Trading posts on Internet forums or through national livebearer organizations are another source for selling your fish. Often this entails your having to ship the fish, using plastic fish bags and a rigid foam board box inside cardboard. The latter are often available via medical offices from the shipment of medicines, and are then discarded.

Your last avenue for selling your fish is through Internet auctions. Here you usually keep most of the profit, but again, shipping must be coordinated. And you are required to sell your fish at the winning bid.

Learning More about Livebearers

Aquarium clubs, the Internet, and this book should put you on a good path to delving into the deep and wonderful world of livebearing fish.

To keep current, a subscription to a monthly aquarium magazine is also recommended. *Tropical Fish Hobbyist* magazine publishes a livebearing fish column every month, as well as special sections and articles on livebearers throughout the year, plus other topics from collection expeditions, filtration, live foods, and many other types of fish. This is a worthy investment because the information here is more timely and vetted by teams of aquarists and editors to ensure accuracy.

Whatever road you take to further your interest in livebearers or any aquarium subject, you will find something that suits your space, time, interest, personality, location, and budget.

The aquarium hobby is truly a great pastime and pleasant respite. Enjoy it and share it with others!

Resources

Magazine

Tropical Fish Hobbyist
1 TFH Plaza
3rd & Union Avenues
Neptune City, NJ 07753
E-mail:info@tfh.com
www.thfmagazine.com

Internet Resources

C.A.R.E.S. Preservation
www.carepreservation.com

FishBase
www.fishbase.org

The Goodeidae Foundation
www.goodeids.org

Goodeiden
www.goodeiden.de

Tropical Resources
www.tropicalresources.net

Viviparous
www.viviparous.org.uk

Wet Web Media
www.wetwebmedia.com

Associations and Societies

American Livebearer Association (ALA)
www.livebearers.org

British Livebearer Association (BLA)
www.britishlivebearerassociation.co.uk

International Fancy Guppy Association (IFGA)
www.ifga.org

Books

Boruchowitz, David E.
Freshwater Aquarium Problem Solver.
TFH Publications, Inc.

Boruchowitz, David E.
Setup & Care of Freshwater Aquariums. TFH Publications, Inc.

Monks, Neale, ed. *Brackish-Water Fishes.* TFH Publications, Inc.

Shubel, Stan. *Aquarium Care of Fancy Guppies.* TFH Publications, Inc.

Ward, Ashley. *Questions and Answers on Freshwater Aquarium Fishes.* TFH Publications, Inc.

Index

Note: **Boldfaced** numbers indicate illustrations; an italic *t* indicates a table.

Dedication

To Veronica, Sabrina, and Travis, who so graciously endure and support all my tanks, all my tubs, and all my writing, all the time.

Acknowledgements

The author would like to thank Craig Sernotti and David Boruchowitz of TFH Publications for their support and input into this project. Acknowledgements are extended to the American Livebearer Association and their library of member information, and members James K. Langhammer (Fellow), Mike Hellweg, Bill Allen, Tom Crane, Larry Jinks, Rit Forcier, and the late Derek Lambert. Thanks also goes out to Ali Shan Aquarium Society of New Jersey for their feedback.

About the Author

Ted Dengler Coletti, Ph.D., has been an aquarium hobbyist for 25 years. He has been writing about tropical fish and the aquarium hobby for the past 17 years. He pens the popular "Livebearers Unlimited" column for *Tropical Fish Hobbyist* Magazine. A former director of the American Livebearer Association, he is one of the founders of the Northeast Livebearer Association, as well as the Aquarium Hobby Historical Society on Yahoo Groups. He has taught courses in aquarium keeping at adult learning campuses, and has presented programs on livebearing fish and water gardens at national aquarium conventions and local aquarium societies throughout the United States. Dr. Ted currently resides in the Skylands region of New Jersey with his wife, children, fish, and guitars.

Photo Credits

Laurence Azoulay: 28, 44, 62; Francine Bethea: 100; Ted Dengler Coletti, Ph.D.: 14, 21, 25, 55, 64, 65, 67, 89, 90 (left & right), 92 (right); Veronica Dengler: 39; Jip Fens (Shutterstock): 13, 32-33, 41, 71; Gary Lange: 36, 102; Horst Linke: 15, 18, 23, 53, 57, 60-61, 68, 82 (right), 87, 92 (left), 95; Oliver Lucanus: 111; William Attard McCarthy (Shutterstock): 30; Kjell Nilsson: 70; Aaron Norman: 12, 73 (right), 79 (top), 86 (right), 98; Dr. Joanne Norton: 47; MP. & C. Piednoir: 4, 22 (top left & right), 26, 33, 50, 73 (left), 82 (left), 83, 86 (left); Hans-Joachim Richter: 78; Andre Roth: 40, 74; Craig Sernotti: 31; Mark Smith: 37, 79 (bottom), 80 (left & right); Stan Sung: 9; Glenn Takeshita: 42; Kenjiro Tanaka: 101; Ed Taylor: 16, 22 (bottom left & right), 45, 63, 77 (left & right), 84, 85, 91, 93, 103; Anthony C. Terceira: 34

All other photos courtesy of the TFH Photo Archives